I0794617

BEHIND THE BIBLE'S GREATEST STORIES

Exploring the Culture, Context, and History of Famous Stories

Paul H. Wright

ROSE PUBLISHING

Behind the Bible's Greatest Stories:
Exploring the Culture, Context, and History of Famous Stories

Published by Rose Publishing
An imprint of Tyndale House Ministries
Carol Stream, Illinois
rose-publishing.com

ISBN: 978-1-4964-8808-4

Author: Paul H. Wright, PhD

Names: Wright, Paul H., Dr author
Title: Behind the Bible's greatest stories : exploring the culture, context, and history of famous stories / Paul H Wright.
Description: First. | Carol Stream, Illinois : Rose Publishing, [2025] | Summary: Commentary for adult readers on seven popular Bible stories from the Old Testament with study questions to facilitate group discussion"- Provided by publisher.
Identifiers: LCCN 2024038720 | ISBN 9781496488084 paperback
Subjects: LCSH: Bible stories | Bible. Old Testament--Commentaries
Classification: LCC BS546 .W745 2025 | DDC 220.95/05--dc23/eng
LC record available at https://lccn.loc.gov/2024038720

Printed in China
December 2024, 1st printing

Contents

INTRODUCTION

THIS BOOK IS about Bible stories. But make no mistake: the stories we will explore are not the ones that sometimes are inflated into tabloid fare or inhabit obscure, less-visited portions of the Bible. No, these are the same stories we once read, or had read to us, as children. Noah and the ark. Moses and the exodus from Egypt. Ruth and Boaz. David and Goliath. Jonah and the whale (or, if you prefer, the big fish). Familiar fare all—or is it?

For centuries the Bible has been the world's most enduring book—and for good reason. It is, first and foremost, inspired Scripture, revealing God's plan of salvation to everyone. But the Bible is also enduring because it is endearing. It speaks to everyone regardless of who we are, our age, gender, ethnicity, nationality, economic status, political persuasion, or social standing, where we live or the century in which we live. And perhaps the most widely known and memorable portions of the Bible are its stories.

Many of the people whom we meet on the pages of Scripture are big characters, familiar to us in their basic storylines. But let's not say, "I've read these stories already" and hurry on to something else. For when we peer a bit deeper, we see that none of the beloved stories of the Bible are quite as simple as they once seemed to us—or perhaps as they still do. In fact, the stories of Scripture are weighty, with characters all too real who act, sometimes, with great faith, but often with the same flaws that plague people everywhere—all laid open and exposed for the world to read. We tend to want to sanitize our favorite Bible characters, make excuses for them (usually through twenty-first century priorities), put halos on them, or rescue them from themselves. It's harder to read their stories and just let them be—juicy details and all.

Because much of the Bible is story, we ought to read with an eye for things that make for good literature: motives and plot; the voice of the narrator and the voices of the characters; foreshadowing, suspense, reversal, and climax; what is said, what is not said, and what is implied. But because these stories record historical events, we should also read them as windows into things that actually happened. As we do, we wonder how we might uncover some of the details about the backstory, information that the authors don't provide. We might also ask what was happening at the time the stories were written that prompted them to be recorded at all.

What we have are records of events, written as stories, in sacred Scripture. Some readers might be happier if the Bible recorded events as cut and dried news accounts, with careful attention to the five *W*s. This might satisfy our urge for knowledge of facts but would probably leave us out of the report ("I'm glad that didn't happen to me!"). Stories draw us in, prompting us to interact and join the drama. They also encourage us to interpret, and this opens the reading process to all manner of response to the claims of the text. Most scholars welcome the task, finding the authority for what the text means in the one reading it. The danger, of course, is that the story then becomes whatever the reader wants it to be. But we are reading divine Scripture and so ought to strive to search out the intent of its authors (and, of course, the divine Author) in whose hands the meaning of the stories resides. The Bible's stories are written for our instruction (2 Tim. 3:16); this is what the word *Torah* means. But rather than providing a list of tight precepts for life, they teach by vivid example.

As we read, the page becomes awash in real life. Inquisitive as we are, we begin to think deeply and to ask questions. Some of our questions are of the "But what actually happened?" type. How big, for instance, was the flood? Where did Moses cross the Red Sea? What did Noah's ark actually look like? What did it take to survive a famine in the ancient world? How many Ninevites actually repented at the words of Jonah? And so on. Things like these we want to know, even if the answers sometimes challenge how we already understand the events of biblical history to have been.

More difficult but equally important are the "But why that way?" questions. Why did Bible people choose to do what they did? What were their intentions and motives? To answer "Because they listened to God" or "Because they were evil" may be right morally and neat theologically, but it doesn't probe very deeply into how conflicted we know people actually are. Motives are often unstated in the biblical storylines, giving readers like us a chance to ferret out reasonable suggestions based on the literary and cultural data available to us, including what we know of the human condition. What did Boaz have to gain by marrying Ruth, a Moabite? Why did Jonah run? Why did Esther agree to enter the pagan king's harem? Could she have said, "Thanks, but no thanks" to the king? What prompted Goliath and his Philistine cohorts to penetrate into Judean territory through the Elah Valley? And why, when they did, did David's father care enough to send his sons down to hold the line? We don't ask questions like these to cast doubt on the biblical accounts but to seek out the whys.

Asking questions helps us think about details not mentioned in biblical stories, details that seem to have been obvious to the writers. Here our search for answers usually takes us to information supplied by cultural studies, archaeology, geography, and written documents from the ancient world other than the Bible. But even so, we must keep in mind that for every insight these aids provide, another question pops up that we likely hadn't thought of yet. And herein lies the root of a host of genuine debates by Bible readers—scholarly and otherwise—about what actually *did* happen in the events that the Bible records as stories. It's easy to read our own context into the actions and motives of the people of the Bible or into the intentions of their authors. It's more difficult to let them act, or write, on their own terms and learn from them rather than mold their thoughts, actions, and motives according to our own understanding of what must have happened and why. Trying to see life the way that the characters and authors of the Bible saw it is one of the most difficult—yet rewarding—parts of reading Bible stories.

Another set of questions prompts us to ask why, or in what way, later biblical authors referred to earlier Bible stories as they wrote their own books that also became Scripture. How, we might ask, did they understand these events? The epistles of Peter, for instance, mention Noah as an illustration of divine judgment yet to come (1 Peter 3:18–22; 2 Peter 2:5; 3:5–6). Several of the psalms sing about Moses and God's triumph in the exodus, reminding Israel that God will continue to be faithful to them as he was to their ancestors (Pss. 68, 77, 78, 80, 81, 99, 105, 106, 114, 135, 136). The prophets, too, encourage Israel to live in ways that are faithful with what it means to be redeemed by appealing to the exodus and wilderness wanderings (Isa. 43:16–20; Ezek. 20:5–10). The book of Proverbs speaks about a "worthy woman," a "woman of noble character" (Prov. 12:4; 31:10). This phrase is used only one other time in the Bible, to describe Ruth (Ruth 3:11). While we are not sure if the book of Ruth was written before Proverbs or vice versa, it is clear that the description of each of these two women helps us understand the other. Bible stories are not meant to be read in isolation from each other or from the rest of Scripture. The primary context for understanding Scripture is Scripture itself. And so as we read, it is worth asking what themes or ideas biblical authors choose to emphasize as they reflect on what earlier biblical stories taught *them*—and what they want to teach us as a result.

This process of reflection hasn't stopped. Bible stories, with loads of fodder for rumination, have been told and retold, shaped and reshaped, adapted, and, yes, even (and eagerly) changed over the centuries. Novelists, bards, musicians, playwrights, pundits, and preachers—not to mention the rest of us—have pulled phrases, characters, and themes off the pages of the Bible and inserted them into a wide variety of songs, sermons, literature, theater productions, movies, commentary, and bedtime stories, all for better and worse.[1] Many of our images of Moses are courtesy of Cecil B. DeMille, and David versus Goliath has become a "little guy beats city hall" idiom. We don't have to look very far to see how the collective heritage of modern culture uses Bible stories to support just about every agenda humanly possible, again for better or worse. All of this can be interesting, but it is more a study of literary malleability, creative history writing, and selective life application than it is reading Bible stories within their own context. It all has value, but in this book we prefer to start with the words of the English hymn writer William Henry Parker, written for his Sunday school students nearly one and a half centuries ago:

Tell me the stories of Jesus I love to hear,
things I would ask him to tell me if he were here:
Scenes by the wayside, tales of the sea,
stories of Jesus, tell them to me.

"Things I would ask him to tell me if he were here." That would be eyewitness accounts, and some of the Bible's authors purport to do exactly that. Their words need to be taken seriously within their own contexts as we strive to find significance in them for our lives today.

Many of the questions prompted by Bible stories are personal, making us think deeply about God, ourselves, and others. How might we best respond to God's claims on our lives, given the complex world in which we live? One helpful way is to see ourselves as one of the characters in a Bible story—and not just the saintly ones. How am I like David, Jonah, or Ruth—or Goliath? As we do, we must keep in mind that it is not fair to expect the people whose stories we read to have the same insights, moral stamina, or theological correctness that we, the readers, have (or think we have), knowing the end of the story before we begin. But if we cut David, Jonah, or Ruth, or even Goliath, some slack as they make their ways through the drama of their lives, we just might be better able to gaze inwardly with more clarity for the effort. One of the best ways that Bible stories invite us in is by leaving us at the door, standing, waiting, in suspense. The book of Jonah, for instance, ends with a question posed by God to the prophet: "Should I not also have compassion on Nineveh?" (Jonah 4:11 NASB). We don't know how Jonah answered, but by not telling us, the author invites us all to ask and then answer the same question for ourselves.

But perhaps the most difficult questions that arise from reading Bible stories are the moral and ethical ones. Are we really to believe that *everyone* deserves to drown in the flood except Noah and his family? Why doesn't Joseph reveal himself to his brothers the first time he sees them in Egypt, rather than act in ways that increase their distress and the distress of his father? Is what Mordecai and Queen Esther do to the Persians justified? Bible characters (even the good ones) tend to try to make a go of things based on what life deals them. (Don't we all.) If they ask God for anything, it is usually to help them do whatever it is they've already planned. Is this the way it's supposed to work when life gets in the way of living? Jacob spends many years of his life believing that his beloved son was ripped to pieces by a wild beast. Naomi loses her entire family in a foreign land. How is that fair? These are difficult questions to raise in Bible storybooks written for children; they're even harder to face once asked by adults. We already know that life is complex. Recognizing complexity in Bible stories makes them more real as we struggle with complexities in our own lives.

As we read through the Bible's stories, we'll see things in them that prompt us to ask difficult questions. Those questions will come to us like Whack-a-Mole: suddenly, unexpectedly; and our answers do sometimes miss. In this book, we won't have time to address everything that pokes up its head—and in any case you will have other questions as you read on your own. I'll suggest answers only sometimes; they may or may not be satisfying to you. But in reading and asking, together we will also learn many things. Mostly, I imagine we would like to learn how to respond better to the claims God has on our lives. His words, preserved for us in Bible stories, are available. And they are meant to be reread. Reading the Bible was never meant to be a one and done. Rather, borrowing words from C. S. Lewis, it is an exercise of going "further up and further in."[2]

I lived in Jerusalem for a quarter century, teaching Bible in context to students who had come to the Holy City from around the world. One of my colleagues was Michael McGarry, head of a Christian study center outside of Bethlehem. Michael is fond of saying, "Tourists who visit the land of Israel differ from pilgrims who make the same journey. Tourists travel through the land; pilgrims allow the land—the locus of God's revelation—to travel through them. Or, to say it differently, tourists ask questions about the land; pilgrims allow the land to ask questions of them." We can say the same thing about those of us who read the Bible, wherever we are. Sometimes we read the Bible as tourists, traveling along its pages and asking questions about what the information found there means. Other times we read as pilgrims, allowing the Bible to work its way through us—asking, compelling, cajoling, and challenging all the way. But one thing that we ought not to do is somehow hope that as we read our way through its pages, the Bible will come alive. According to Hebrews 4:12, the Bible *already* is alive: it's "living and active." Rather, we read the Bible so that *it* can enliven *us*. That's the end goal of a journey in reading that is worth taking.

Notes

1 For examples, see David Lyle Jeffrey, gen. ed., *A Dictionary of Biblical Tradition in English Literature* (Eerdmans, 1992).

2 C. S. Lewis, *The Last Battle* (Collier Books, 1970), 165. Lewis uses the phrase to describe our ever-growing knowledge and fulfillment of heaven once we enter eternal life.

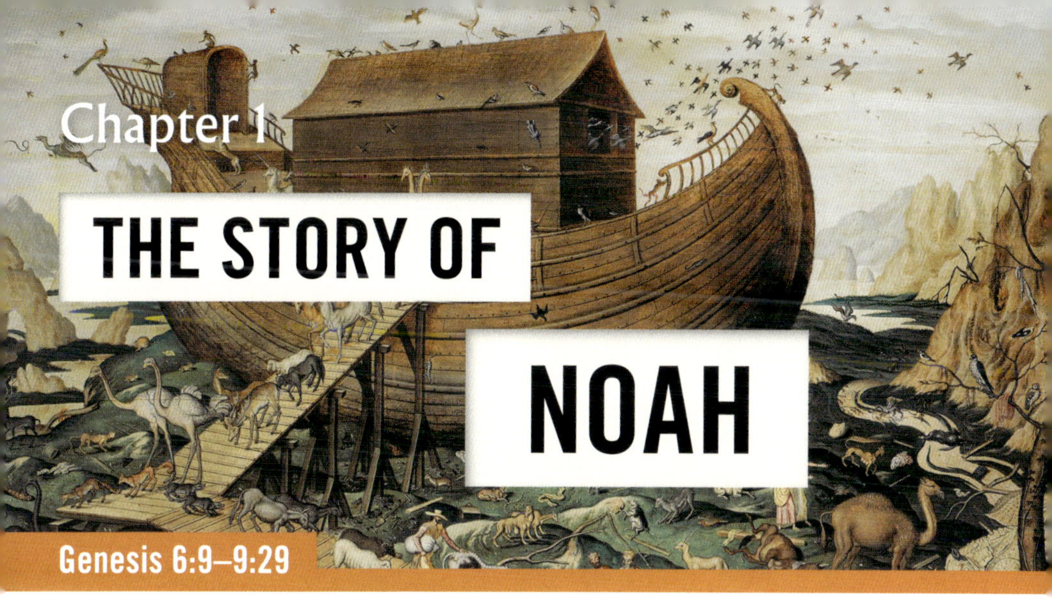

Chapter 1

THE STORY OF NOAH

Genesis 6:9–9:29

THE STORY OF Noah is so well known that even those of us who are otherwise totally unfamiliar with the Bible resonate with its characters, the animals, and, of course, the ark. But what for many has become just a cute children's tale is already in the earliest chapters of the Bible a pivotal narrative revealing something fundamental about the nature of people and of God. The story fills nearly a third of the primeval (pre-Abraham) history recorded in Genesis. For this reason, it is difficult to treat it as a stand-alone account and still grasp the full impact of the consequences of the flood, God's means of salvation through the ark, and our response. Indeed, the story of Noah is a story for people of all ages, and the older and more biblically astute we grow, the more perplexing, demanding, and compelling it becomes.

Details about the extent of the flood, the size of the ark, the number and kind of animals on board, and Noah's subsequent drunkenness are all interesting parts of the narrative, but they are not its primary message. Rather, Noah's ark and the flood are the frame that allows the message of the story to be seen. Through the details of the Noah story we are able to glimpse something tangible about who God is and what his relationship with creation, especially people, entails.

The truths about the character of God and people are magnified when we compare Noah's story with other ancient Near Eastern stories of floods sent by gods to destroy humanity. These stories reflect the polytheistic worldview out of which God called Noah to save humanity—and then later Abraham to be a blessing to the world (Gen. 12:1–3). The flood stories from Mesopotamia are parts of longer compositions that speak about the gods and their unfavorable attitude toward people. They seem to have been written to justify the actions of kings or priests wanting to subdue the commotion of their own noisy subjects.

- A Sumerian story tells of Ziusudra, a pious king who overheard a plan of the gods to destroy humankind by a flood. Ziusudra saved himself in a boat and offered a sacrifice to the gods after the flood; then he was given eternal life.
- The Old Babylonian Atra-hasis epic relates how the gods sent a seven-day flood to silence people on an over-crowded earth from making noise that bothered them. Atra-hasis was saved by building a reed boat and taking some animals with him.
- The Babylonian Gilgamesh epic includes a flood story telling how Utnapishtim escaped a seven-day flood sent by the gods, ostensibly to punish people. This so-called "Babylonian Noah" took all living things with him onto a reed boat sealed with pitch to ride out the flood, which came as a violent thunderstorm. Utnapishtim used birds to check if the water had receded and offered a sacrifice upon disembarking; then he was given eternal life by the gods. (This is the most complete Mesopotamian flood story.)

Gilgamesh Epic, Tablet 11, which mentions Utnapishtim's flood

Because these flood stories have many similar details, scholars often conclude that they are local variations of a common memory, tracing them to an original story about the king of Shuruppak, a prominent city in southern Mesopotamia.

Together, these versions show us that the polytheistic worldview of ancient Mesopotamia was a belief system which differed widely in essential ways from the revelation of God that is recorded in the Bible. For the pagan world, the flood was an event caused by capricious deities intent on protecting their own comfort and interests. In the Gilgamesh epic, the gods even hid their coming judgment from people so as to try to not give anyone a chance to survive. In the Bible, the flood is an act of moral judgment followed by grace with the intent of restoring wholeness, fellowship, and peace between people and God. Even though Noah's story and the Mesopotamian flood stories share some similarities (not surprising since they're from the same ancient geographical location), there are significant foundational differences about God's character and his relationship with people that we read in the biblical account, things that are lacking in flood stories of the nations from whom God chose to redeem people.

The Ancient Near East (3rd millennium BC)

Themes in the Story of Noah

God exists, is sovereign, and has the right to govern creation in any way that he sees fit.

We see this theme in two ways.

Firstly, even though the story of the flood tells us many things that Noah did, it is not a story about him but about God. Nor is this primarily a story about God sending a flood but about why he saves Noah. The answer has to do with Noah's character, and we can infer something about that from his actions in the story. Like Adam and Enoch, Noah "walked with God" and was "a righteous man, blameless in his generation" (Gen. 6:9; cf. Gen. 3:8; 5:24; Ezek. 14:14, 20). And while the story does not mention why God considers Noah to be righteous (is it his actions or attitude?), Noah's character is proven to be such as the events of his story unfold. "He did all," we read repeatedly, "that God commanded him" (Gen. 6:22; cf. 7:5, 9, 16). Yet strangely enough, Noah himself never says anything in the biblical text. As a result, we lack Noah's own voice about the situation of his day, his inmost hopes and fears, and even his own motives and attitudes for doing what he did. It is only much later that the writer of Hebrews gives us a clue: Noah acted "by faith" and "in reverent fear"; that is, his faith was proven to be valid by his actions, which were done with all due reverence and respect to God (Heb. 11:7). Because Noah never speaks, we must consider him a silent character, someone who acts but is not the one driving the action. The one who does speak, and at all the key moments, is God—even to the extent of providing blueprints for the ark (Gen. 6:14–16). Throughout, it is God's words that hold power, express revelation, and define who Noah is and what he will become.

Secondly, we see that God is sovereign because the flood is depicted as a reversal of creation. In Genesis 1, God separates the chaotic waters of the cosmic deep so that dry ground appears, ground that becomes fertile and full of life as the days of creation unfold. God calls this created land "good"—that is, a place suitable for humans to live (Gen. 1:10, 12, 18, 21, 25, 31). With the flood, a few chapters later in Genesis, the mass of waters again overwhelms the earth, taking away fertile ground and the possibility of life with it. The God who chooses to create can also choose to de-create if he so wishes (Jer. 4:23–26; 2 Peter 3:5–7).

Humans fail in their responsibility to live in righteous, helpful ways before God and others.

God plants the tree of the knowledge of good and evil in the middle of the garden of Eden, then prohibits Adam and Eve from eating from it so that they (and we) will understand that it is God the creator, not people, who determine what is good for human life (Gen. 2:9; 3:5). But Eve, and then Adam, do indeed eat, and ever since then the natural tendency to choose what is wrong instead of what is right has been a principal attribute of what it means to be human (Gen. 3:1–24; Jer. 17:5–10).

The story of Noah displays the full force of human depravity: the consequence of wanting to usurp the rights and character of God (Gen. 3:22; 6:5). On the question, "Are people inherently good or evil?," the story of Noah clearly teaches the latter. Just a few generations from creation, the earth and all its people are already "corrupt … and … filled with violence" (Gen. 6:11–12). These are words that reveal the rapid advancement of sin in all contexts: things affecting the body, mind, and spirit; things both done and left undone; things of the individual; things of society; and things of the world.

Judgment of human sin is certain, and it reveals a significant part of the character of God.

Writing much later, after Israel has been exiled to Babylon, the prophet Ezekiel declares that even if God had sent Noah, Daniel, and Job to Jerusalem, these men would have been able to save only themselves since they, and no one else, was righteous in their day (Ezek. 14:14, 20). For Ezekiel, the flood is seen as a forerunner of the judgment of God on the kingdom of Judah of his day. But the judgment of the flood also foreshadows an even greater judgment by God at the end of time (Matt. 24:36–39; 2 Peter 2:1–10; 3:3–7). As we begin working our way through the Bible with the accounts of Genesis, we might think it rather unfair that the whole thing opens on such a stark note. But the biblical authors know life too well to pull punches or offer a goody-goody hope to their readers. God's right to judge pervades the message of the Bible, yes, but it is always accompanied by the reality of his grace and willingness to save, even if it be only a faithful a remnant like the family of Noah.

We need to wait for God to act.

Though not always explicitly stated in Genesis, the timeline of the flood implies that Noah and his family, a remnant of only eight people out of everyone on earth, repeatedly wait for God to act:

- they wait for the rain to start after the door of the ark is closed (Gen. 7:9–10);
- they wait for the waters of the flood to subside after the rain has stopped (Gen. 8:1–5);
- they wait as a raven and then a dove take flight to see if the land can support life yet (Gen. 8:6–12); and
- they wait for God's command before coming out of the ark (Gen. 8:13–19).

In the face of the persistent question, "Why is God silent in an enraged world?," the story of Noah demonstrates that God knows the right time to act (1 Peter 3:20). He also knows the extent to which he must act. The picture of a faithful remnant waiting for God, a God who often seems to remain behind the scenes, sets the tone for later stories about his people waiting for deliverance: those under the bondage of pharaoh in Egypt (Ex. 2:23–25); the remnant of Israel in exile in Babylon (Lam. 3:26); the psalmist imploring a silent God (Pss. 37:34; 38:15; 40:1); and believers waiting for the coming of the divine Messiah, the Son of Man, who will set the world aright (Matt. 24:36–44). Jesus compares the coming of the Son of Man to the days of Noah: "Just as it was in the days of Noah, so will it be in the days of the Son of Man. They were eating and drinking and marrying and being given in marriage, until the day when Noah entered the ark, and the flood came and destroyed them all" (Luke 17:26–27). God withholds his hand of judgment for such a long time that people act as if it will never come. God's reticence to act quickly is not a measure of his indifference or inability to act, but of his grace.

The hope of salvation is certain—and with it the ability to start over.

The writer of Genesis says that "the Lord was sorry that He had made mankind" (Gen. 6:6 NASB), but he also notes that Noah's father names his son Noah because he will "bring … relief" to a toilsome world (Gen. 5:28–29). The Hebrew verbs "to be sorry" and "to bring relief" both come from the same root (*n-u-ḥ*), which in essence means "to be moved to pity." The name Noah may come from the same root or from a different Hebrew root that means "to rest, be at rest, or settle down" (*n-ḥ-m*). Both meanings are reflected in the story, and like so many biblical characters, Noah is aptly named.

And so the story of Noah begins with hope, found in God's choice of someone who will be delivered because of his righteousness and obedience. This introduces a wonderfully persistent biblical theme: there is a faithful remnant that God saves from judgment (Isa. 10:20–23; 46:3–4; 2 Chron. 36:22–23; Rom. 11:5–6). The first epistle of Peter compares the flood to the waters of baptism, which also signal salvation to a new life (1 Peter 3:18–22).

In the story of Noah, new life—and with it the ability to start over—is carefully depicted as a second creation (being "created again," as it were), setting the world back to the way it was first supposed to be:

- God pushes the waters away by a *ruah*, translated "Spirit" in the creation account of Genesis 1:2 and "wind" as the flood recedes in Genesis 8:1.
- The birds and animals that exit the ark are described in ways that remind us of the categories of birds and animals at creation (Gen. 1:20–25; 8:17, 19).

- God reiterates that people will still have authority—we should assume respectful, not malicious or manipulative, authority—over all animals, birds, and fish (Gen. 1:26–29; 9:2–4).
- Even after the flood, people are still made in the image of God, with the mandate to be fruitful, multiply, and increase upon the earth (Gen. 1:22, 27–28; 8:17; 9:1, 6–7).
- In creation, God plants a garden (Gen. 2:8), and after the flood, Noah plants a vineyard—a type of garden in a world renewed (Gen. 9:20). Both are places of life and blessing; both become the setting of sin.

Events in the Story of Noah

The Coming Storm GENESIS 6:9–22

God tells Noah to build the ark in order to survive a flood which will destroy all human and animal life on the earth. He then tells Noah how to make the ark and to bring animals and food on board. Noah does as God commands.

The story of Noah begins with a plan—not Noah's plan but God's. The Lord reveals to Noah the coming calamity, and he explains what Noah should do to survive it. Then the narrator tells us, simply, "Noah did this" (Gen. 6:22). What the storyteller does not tell us is exactly when Noah begins to build the ark, how he gains the necessary engineering expertise to do so, who helps him (if anyone), how he can afford to build it, or how long it takes to do so. The popular suggestions that Noah and his sons were ridiculed by their neighbors and that Noah spent time warning people far and wide about God's upcoming judgment appear only in Jewish and Christian texts from the time of the New Testament or later.[1] The epistle of 2 Peter, roughly contemporary to many of these, calls Noah "a herald of righteousness" but provides no details to explain the phrase (2 Peter 2:5).

In Noah's story, the Hebrew word for ark, *tevah*, is an Egyptian loan word that means "chest." This word is used in only one other place in the Bible: for the closed basket in which the infant Moses is placed to float safely in the waters of the Nile (Ex. 2:3–6; the word for the *ark* of the covenant is a different term: *'aron*). Noah's ark is made of *gopher* wood, a Hebrew term that is understood to be either cypress, oak, cedar, willow, or a different wood altogether—the particular kind remains a matter of debate. Like the papyrus ark that cradles Moses in the Nile, the joints of Noah's ark are sealed with pitch (bitumen). Some scholars have suggested that the timbers and planks of Noah's ark were sewn together by fiber ropes rather than fastened with pegs, a boatbuilding practice known in ancient Egypt and attested along the Indian Ocean for thousands of years.

Building the Ark
(James Tissot, c. 1896-1902)

The dimensions of the ark are given in cubits, a unit of length that varied in the ancient world but was approximately 18 inches (46 cm). The ark was 300 cubits (450 ft; 130 m) long, 50 cubits (75 ft; 23 m) wide, and 30 cubits (45 ft; 13.5 m) high, giving a length to width dimension of 6:1, which is considered to be the dimension for a stable vessel today. The ark was significantly larger than any other known vessel in the ancient world or, for that matter, any boat until the late nineteenth century AD.

Genesis 6:16 is a difficult verse to translate: "Make a roof for the ark, and finish it to a cubit above, and set the door of the ark in its side. Make it with lower, second, and third decks." This is usually taken to indicate that the ark had a single door in the hull, a row of relatively small windows just under the roofline, and three decks containing rooms. The Babylonian Talmud, a Jewish legal document dating to the early sixth century AD that codified centuries of oral tradition, reports that the bottom deck held manure, the middle deck was for animals, and the top deck provided living space for people.[2] This is as good an estimation of floor use as any suggestion since.

The Animals GENESIS 7:1–9

Noah, his family, two pairs of every unclean animal and seven pairs of every clean animal enter the ark. Noah is 600 years old.

In Genesis 7, we find a curious detail about the animals Noah takes into the ark: he brings more "clean" animals than "not clean" ones (vv. 2–3). According to Leviticus 11 and Deuteronomy 14:4–20, clean animals are those that are suitable (kosher) for sacrifice in the temple and for human consumption. But why the distinction between clean and unclean animals already in the story of Noah? How does Noah know which animals are clean, since he lives long before the instructions of Leviticus and Deuteronomy?[3] Noah is not given any restrictions after the flood regarding which animals are suitable as food ("*Every* moving thing that lives shall be food for you," Gen. 9:3, emphasis added). Nothing in the story tells us that Noah understands why God makes this distinction between clean and unclean animals as cargo (we certainly cannot expect him to have anticipated future regulations for sacrifice). Rather, it all seems to be another example of Noah's obedience to God's command, whether he fully understood the *why* behind the command or not.

The story of Noah does not provide details about any of the practical considerations regarding the animals, birds, and "every creeping thing of the ground" that are in the ark. Questions—and speculations—abound:

- The animals, birds, and creeping things are "according to its kind" (Gen. 6:19–20). Because we do not know if *kind* refers to species or a different category of animals, we cannot know how many animals in total are on the ark. The word *kind* is also used in the first chapter of Genesis to describe the animals, birds, and creeping things that God made on days five and six of creation (Gen. 1:21,

24). This helps us see the flood as a reversal and then a renewal of creation.

- There is no indication as to the actual process by which the animals come to Noah, especially those living excessively far away (Gen. 6:20; 7:8–9, 15). Nor should we expect them to enter the ark in a neat double column, pair after docile pair, as picture books so richly illustrate.
- How might the animals be kept healthy (other than fed; Gen. 6:21) and docile, especially the non-domesticated ones? Are eight people—Noah, his wife, his three sons and their wives—enough to care for all of them?
- How old are the animals? Apparently old enough and sufficiently healthy, once the waters subside, to reproduce.
- Did any reproduce or perish during the journey?

Noah Leading the Animals into the Ark (Giovanni Benedetto Castiglione, c. 1645)

Silence in the story about these and other questions has led to many suggestions and dramatizations about the menagerie of Noah's ark. As early as the end of the first millennium BC, Jewish texts, followed by the early church fathers, elaborated the story to fill in some of the blanks. For instance, the Babylonian Talmud offers fanciful stories under the memory of a supposed eyewitness: "We experienced great suffering in the ark caring for the animals"—feeding by day those that eat by day and feeding by night those that eat by night. The lion, the Talmud tells us, had a fever and so wouldn't eat for a week, giving some relief to the overburdened caregivers, while the phoenix(!) said that it would help by dying and then coming back to life as the ark landed.[4] The church father Augustine of Hippo wondered if perhaps Noah brought additional animals onto the ark to serve as food for the carnivores (he mentions lions and eagles in particular) or if he brought some sort of meat substitute instead. Augustine also wondered if provision for the lions and eagles was something that Noah thought of or if God specifically told him to do it.[5] The point is not so much what Augustine suggested, but that he, too, pondered questions that the story itself does not clearly answer. More recently, some interpreters have suggested that the animals hibernated in the ark or didn't eat much because they were small (though for most of the animal kingdom a year's growth—the length of time that everyone is aboard—is quite substantial). Others suggest that the land surface of the earth differed before the flood, making it easier to collect animals from places now separated by water, irrespective of the speed of movement. (Maybe the sloths got a head start.)

Nothing in the biblical text is said about fish, even though a massive flood would have wreaked havoc with saltwater and freshwater habitats. Nor is anything said about plants, most of which would have been destroyed by the flood as well, or how they sprang back to life after a full year's inundation. But one thing the story does provide is a very exact reckoning of the passage of time from one event to another, more so than any other story in the Bible. In doing so, it anchors in real time events that otherwise seem larger than life. Yet the dates in the story are not given according to a system with specific month names keyed to an established civilization but are instead reckoned according to Noah's age: "Noah was six hundred years old when …" (Gen. 7:6; cf. Gen. 5:32; 7:11; 8:13). This suggests that Noah can be viewed as the founder of a new humanity, practically as well as morally.

NOAH'S LONG LIFE

Genesis records that Noah lived 950 years (Gen. 9:29), while his father Lamech lived 777 years (Gen. 5:31) and his grandfather Methuselah, 969 years (Gen. 5:27). Scholars have offered several suggestions for the long lifespans of people born prior to the flood. While some accept these numbers at face value, others suggest that they represent the length of family lines, are literary exaggerations, or reflect different methods of counting, such as using base 6 rather than base 10 as is standard for computation today.[6] Whatever it was, Genesis indicates that lifespans gradually shortened in the generations following the flood (Gen. 11:10–26).

The Fountains of the Deep GENESIS 7:10–24

After waiting on the battened-down ark for seven days, rain falls for forty days and forty nights. The ensuing flood covers the earth for 150 days.

With Noah, his family, and the animals securely inside the ark, the flood starts when "all the fountains of the great deep burst forth, and the windows of the heavens were opened," and this continues for "forty days and forty nights" (Gen. 7:11–12). Forty is a common number for indicating intervals of time in the Bible: for example, the three phases of Moses's life; the time of wilderness wanderings; the length of peace after each judge; the years of the reigns of Saul, David, and Solomon; and the days of Jesus's temptation. This pattern suggests that forty may be a round or approximate number for reckoning time or used symbolically.

Genesis 7:19 tells us that "the waters prevailed so mightily on the earth that all the high mountains under the whole heaven were covered." It is possible to explain the presence of subterranean waters sufficient for a flood that covers the highest mountains on earth to a depth of 15 cubits (20 ft; 6 m; Gen. 7:20) and the waters disappearing after the flood only if we assume that there was a very different geological structure prior to the flood than is present today, as some interpreters do. While many interpreters hold that certain geological features of the earth today were caused by a massive flood in ancient times, most portions of the globe show no evidence of significant flooding and much of the earth's geological structure (such as stratification) cannot be explained adequately by a single flood. In any case, arguments for a worldwide flood based on geology are strongest if the existence of current geological structures cannot be explained by any other means.

A few cities in Mesopotamia, where scholars usually suggest Noah might have lived, show archaeological evidence of having been inundated by a massive flood (e.g., Ur, Uruk, Shuruppak, Lagash, Kish, and Nineveh), though at different times over the fourth and third millennia BC. This is not surprising since these cities lay in the flood plain of the Tigris and Euphrates rivers. Most ancient cities in the area, however, reveal no indication of having been flooded, nor do the vast majority of ancient cities around the globe. For this reason, archaeological evidence for a worldwide flood is lacking.

Tigris River and flood plain, Iraq

By some calculations there are nearly three hundred flood stories from across the globe. Most come from the Pacific Islands, Australia, the Americas, and some parts of Asia, with a few from Africa and Europe. It is possible to emphasize items of similarity between them and conclude that they point to a worldwide flood. It is also possible to maintain that they cannot point to a single event because they differ widely in many significant details. In any case, since devastating local floods were a common occurrence, it is only reasonable that memory of at least some of them would have been preserved in local stories.

The best evidence for understanding the extent of the flood is the text of Genesis itself, although even here the language of Scripture is open to interpretation. In normal speech, a word or phrase can be used both literally and as an idiom, with either correct in any given situation. The same is true in the Bible. For example, the term *all*, which indicates how many high mountains on earth were covered by the floodwaters (Gen. 7:19) as well as the number of people whom God promises to never destroy by a flood again (Gen. 9:11), is used to refer to only a limited portion of the earth in Genesis 41:57: "All the earth came to Egypt to Joseph to buy grain." Geographical terms in the Bible nearly always describe features within view of the author's or characters' own known world. In this case, "all the high mountains under the whole heaven" would indicate that the mountains which were covered with water were most reasonably those within the purview of Noah. Similarly, the geographical phrase "mountains of Ararat" on which the ark landed includes not just the highest peak labeled Ararat by modern cartographers but also the surrounding lower foothills and range (Gen. 8:4). The Hebrew term translated as *covered* ("all the high mountains under the whole heaven were covered," Gen. 7:19) can mean "drenched with" as is its sense in Malachi 2:13 ("You cover the LORD's altar with tears"), as well as "submerged by." And the Hebrew term for *earth* that is used repeatedly in the flood story is not *tevel*, meaning "globe," but *eretz*, a word that can mean "earth" but typically just means "land," something within the known world of those witnessing an event. On the other hand, the Hebrew term for the flood, *mabbul*, is something quite special, a word used only in the story of Noah and in Psalm 29:10. We get our English word *cataclysm* from the corresponding Greek term, *kataklysmos*, an indication that the flood was indeed cataclysmic for everyone involved, irrespective of its actual extent.

If we read the geographical terms in the story in a way that allows for a local rather than universal flood (which the language allows though doesn't demand), then it seems likely that the flood was not meant to kill everyone on earth but instead a number large enough to serve as an example to the rest. Then again, if the flood were local, why not just hike to the highest hill beyond its reach and skip the ark altogether? That, of course, wouldn't make for much of a story. The crux of the question "How big was the flood?" is one embedded in the biblical text itself, not the disciplines of archaeology or geology, and the significant issue is "Can the text be truthful either way?" Based on how all languages work, the answer has to be yes. For this reason, questions of theology or the inspiration of Scripture, including the understanding that Jesus had about the flood (Matt. 24:37–39), ought not be affected by the issue of the flood's physical extent.

To summarize, it seems as though the arguments advanced for either a universal flood or a local flood based on archaeology, geology, or the text of Genesis are not watertight. In principle, science should not dictate what a text (other than a scientific treatise) should or should not mean. Rather, science deals with physical realities about which a text can choose to speak on its own terms.

Leaving the Ark GENESIS 8:1–19

The flood stops, and as the waters begin to recede, the ark comes to rest on the mountains of Ararat. Noah sends a raven from the ark, then sends doves four times to see if they can find dry land. He, his family, and the animals leave the ark after the earth is dry.

When God "remember[s]" Noah and all the animals on the ark (Gen. 8:1), he brings the floodwaters of divine judgment to an end. The ark runs aground "on the mountains of Ararat," a plural term that indicates the massive, rugged Ararat range which dominates the region of Lake Van in the eastern, Armenian, portion of Turkey (Gen. 8:4; cf. 2 Kings 19:37; Isa. 37:38; Jer. 51:27). The highest peak of the range, labeled Mount Ararat today, is 16,854 feet (5137 m) in elevation. Expeditions to find remains of the ark had already begun in antiquity. In the late first century AD, the Jewish historian Josephus mentioned several other Greek writers who reported that in his day the site of the ark was still known in the mountains of Armenia (eastern Turkey).[7] He added that the Armenians living there showed relics of the ark and that people would cart off pieces of its timber and bitumen as souvenirs. While it is not possible to verify these ancient accounts (they sound fanciful), pilots during World War II reported seeing the shape of an ark in the same general area, reviving interest in the hunt. Unstable political conditions, harsh landscapes, and a brutal climate have all conspired to hinder easy exploration, yet some who have braved the call claim, with great fanfare, to have found the remains of Noah's ark. None of these alleged sightings have been properly verified or gained general—not to mention scholarly—acceptance.

On the dove's third trip from the ark, it plucks a fresh leaf from an olive tree (Gen. 8:11). The olive tree is an evergreen and exceptionally hardy in that it can survive the harsh growing conditions found throughout the Middle East. It cannot, however, survive having been totally inundated for an entire year. Nor can this leaf have come from wholly new growth, since an olive seed needs several years to grow into a tree sufficiently leafed for a bird to be attracted to it. Both of these considerations, together with a recognition that there is nothing in the story that hints that the olive tree was preserved by a special miracle by God, suggest that the flood covered all of the land that was within the known world, or purview, of Noah, but not the entire globe.

Olives remain a dietary staple across the world of the Bible.

Scientific considerations aside, what's more significant in the biblical storyline is what the olive leaf represents. Throughout the Bible the olive tree, its leaves, and its oil are indications of God's favor, blessing, life, and peace (e.g., Deut. 7:13; Judg. 9:9; Ps. 128:3; Isa. 61:3; Jer. 31:12). The God who created all life in Genesis 1 is the same God who brings forth new growth in Genesis 8—a new creation has dawned.

Durupinar, a flat "ark-shaped" site (nestled in the center-right of this picture) in the Ararat foothills, popularized in the 1980s as a location for Noah's ark, though any evidence for the ark here is yet to be found.

The Covenant GENESIS 8:20–9:17

Noah builds an altar to the Lord and sacrifices animals on it. God makes a covenant with Noah that he will never again destroy all humanity by a flood, sealing it with the sign of a rainbow.

As the story draws to a conclusion, we are struck broadside by Noah's burnt offering. Those poor animals, saved only to be sacrificed! For an entire year they are cared for by Noah through a cataclysmic flood, only to be killed by him as soon as they leave the ark. Every other living thing finds a new home; they find death instead. Here the power of sacrifice, raw emotion mixed with the force of shed blood, is on full display. The world starts anew, but the human condition hasn't changed. The time after the flood may well be re-creation, but it isn't a return to Eden.

Many interpreters have understood God's permission that Noah can eat animals, birds, and fish as an indication that prior to the flood, he intended people to be vegetarians (Gen. 9:2–3; cf. 1:29–30). Others note that while at creation God gave plants as food to "everything that has the breath of life," he didn't specifically forbid either people or animals from eating meat (Gen. 1:30). The provision of plants as food doesn't necessarily imply prohibition of animals as food. In any case, like the distinction between clean and unclean animals, God's command in Genesis 9:4 that Noah "not eat flesh with its life, that is, its blood" is consistent with the laws of proper diet and food preparation given in Leviticus (Lev. 7:26; 17:10–13; 19:26). These provide a basis for kosher food laws observed by Jews still today.

Genesis 9:8–17 is the first use of the word *covenant* (*berit*) in the Bible. Although the details of the various covenants in the Old Testament differ, all carry the intent of restoring fellowship with people and bringing people back to God. The covenant in Noah's story is an everlasting covenant, made with him by God on behalf of all humanity and hence detailing principles for life that are proper for everyone. Noah's covenant focuses on the innate value of human life based on the realization that even after the flood, people are still made in the image of God (Gen. 9:6). In the Bible's prophetic literature, the rainbow symbolizes the radiance and majesty of God and his angels (Ezek. 1:28; Rev. 4:3; 10:1). In the story of Noah, it is the visible seal of God's covenant that he will not destroy all life on earth by flood again.

Noah Offering a Sacrifice of Gratitude (Joseph Anton Koch, c. 1803)

Noah's Shame GENESIS 9:18–29

Noah plants a vineyard, gets drunk, and responds by cursing and blessing his sons.

The final episode in the Noah story shows that human sinfulness continues in spite of the judgments and blessings of God, and despite the second chance for life that is given to humanity after the flood. It sets the tone—and need—for the ongoing revelation of redemption that unfolds in the rest of the Bible.

While the story of Noah's nakedness and Ham's actions has received a great deal of attention in literature and preaching through the centuries—most of it focused on a variety of sordid behaviors—there is nothing in the text to suggest anything specific about what actually happened or what the motives of either Noah or his sons were. Nakedness in the Bible often indicates shame arising from something that already happened; it is generally not a condition to tempt people to sin. Nor can we conclude that Noah's curse of Ham's son Canaan, whatever its ramifications were at the time (Gen. 9:25; cf. 10:1, 15), carries implications for Canaan's descendants for all time in light of God's promise that all the peoples of the world can be blessed through Abraham (Gen. 12:3). What we do see in the story of Noah's nakedness is that the response of Ham, who sees and tattles about it, and that of Shem and Japheth who cover Noah up, represent the two choices that everyone makes when confronted with guilt and shame; it can be ignored, or absolved.

Mt. Ararat (background, right) towers over a vineyard in the Ararat valley.

NOAH IN LATER WRITINGS

When later biblical writers mention Noah, they do so in the context of salvation from judgment to come. This supports the idea that the point of the story of Noah is not about details of the ark or the flood but about the character of God and his interaction with people. These and similar themes are frequent topics in early Jewish writings roughly contemporary with the Gospels:

- In the *Apocalypse of Adam*, Noah defends himself before God for giving birth to a line of descendants who were just as corrupt as those who perished in the flood.[8]
- In *1 Enoch*, God speaks to a Noah figure, Asuryal, and tells him to escape a coming flood by fleeing, rather than building an ark. The text then explains that the corrupt deeds that brought about the flood were done by people who had learned the secret powers of angels and demons.[9]
- The *Sibylline Oracles* includes a lengthy speech by Noah calling on everyone to repent of their wicked ways; here the misdeeds are more pedestrian: violence, shedding blood, drunkenness, anger, immodesty, adultery, and slander.[10]
- Pseudo-Philo specifies the kinds of judgments that God will bring about in latter days instead of another flood: famine, war, fire, death, earthquakes, and dispersion to uninhabited lands.[11]
- In the book of *Jubilees*, Noah is the first person to keep the feast of Weeks (Shavuot, or Pentecost) and the first one to use herbs for healing.[12]

In the New Testament, Noah serves as an example of salvation by faith and a warning about God's final judgment on humanity (Heb. 11:7; 1 Peter 3:20; 2 Peter 2:5). As for the church fathers, Noah is often an example of obedience or a new Adam, a forerunner of Christ:

- Justin Martyr (second century AD) taught that Noah was a figure of Christ, someone who was saved to new life through water (the flood, and baptism), faith, and wood (the ark, and the cross).[13]
- John Chrysostom (fourth century AD) wrote that God chose Noah

because the conduct of his life showed him to be trustworthy with regard to all of God's commands.[14]

- Ambrose of Milan (fourth century AD) added that whereas many people may appear righteous by their deeds, God saw that Noah was indeed righteous because of the truth of his virtue and the purity of his soul.[15]

The trend to focus on these and similar themes has continued in classical English literature where all manner of Noah-like characterizations appear. For example, Noah becomes a carpenter who fears a second flood (Chaucer, *Miller's Tale*); a purveyor of judgment and logic (Shakespeare, *Twelfth Night*); and, following the church fathers, a new Adam and type of Christ (Milton, *Paradise Lost*). More frequently, classical novelists have parodied Noah's drunkenness and fondness for wine (foibles make for juicer reading than right living). By comparison, treatises on how the biblical record relates to modern science with reference to the cause, extent, and results of the flood have appeared only in the last century.

Study Questions

1. What are some ways that the story of Noah differs from flood stories of ancient Mesopotamia? What do these differences tell us about the nature and character of God?
2. Would your understanding of God's judgment and his grace be different if the events of the story of Noah happened today rather than in the distant past? If so, how?
3. Consider this statement: "God's reticence to act quickly is not a measure of his indifference or inability to act, but of his grace." When you think about today's world, do you agree with this statement? Why or why not?
4. Do you think the flood was literally worldwide or far more localized? In terms of what the story of Noah teaches us about God and people, does it make a difference whether the flood was worldwide or local?
5. Give some examples of how modern retellings of the story of Noah have added to it to fill in some things the biblical author doesn't mention. Then give some examples of things that the author does mention which modern readers tend to skip over or ignore.
6. The story of Noah ends where it began, with human sinfulness and individual choice. What does this teach us about the nature and character of people—and of God?

Chapter 1 Notes

1 Josephus, *Antiquities of the Jews,* i.74; *Sibylline Oracles* 1:147–198; Babylonian Talmud, *Sanhedrin,* 108b; and various writings of Augustine, among others.
2 Babylonian Talmud, *Sanhedrin,* 108b.
3 Many scholars suggest that the Noah story was written after the laws of clean and unclean foods were established and that he was then portrayed as keeping these laws in order to be considered fully righteous.
4 Babylonian Talmud, *Sanhedrin,* 108b.
5 Augustine of Hippo, Question 6 on Genesis.
6 Sexagesimal (base 6) mathematics was used in ancient Babylon and by the Sumerians as early as the third millennium BC. Modern remnants include the 360-degree circle and the practice of dividing the hour into sixty minutes.
7 Josephus, *Antiquities of the Jews,* i.92–95.
8 *Apocalypse of Adam,* 3:11–16.
9 *1 Enoch* 10:1–3; 65:6.
10 *Sibylline Oracles,* 1:147–198.
11 Pseudo-Philo 3:9.
12 *Jubilees* 6:17–19; 10:10–13.
13 Justin Martyr, *Dialogue with Trypho,* CXXXVIII.
14 John Chrysostom, Homiletic 24 on Genesis.
15 Ambrose of Milan, *Noah and the Ark,* 11.37.

Chapter 1 Images

Noah's Ark on the Mount Ararat by Simon de Myle, 1570
Gilgamesh Epic, Tablet 11, found on the citadel mound of Nineveh, The British Museum (Mike Peel/Wikimedia)
The Ancient Near East, satellite map courtesy of NASA
Building the Ark by James Tissot, c. 1896–1902, The Jewish Museum
Noah Leading the Animals into the Ark by Giovanni Benedetto Castiglione, c. 1645, National Gallery of Art
Tigris River (Lena Ha/Shutterstock)
Olive tree (Paul H. Wright)
Durupinar site, Agri Province, Turkey (Inna Giliarova/Shutterstock)
Landscape with Noah Offering a Sacrifice of Gratitude by Joseph Anton Koch, c. 1803, Städel Museum
Mount Ararat (Goinyk Production/Shutterstock)

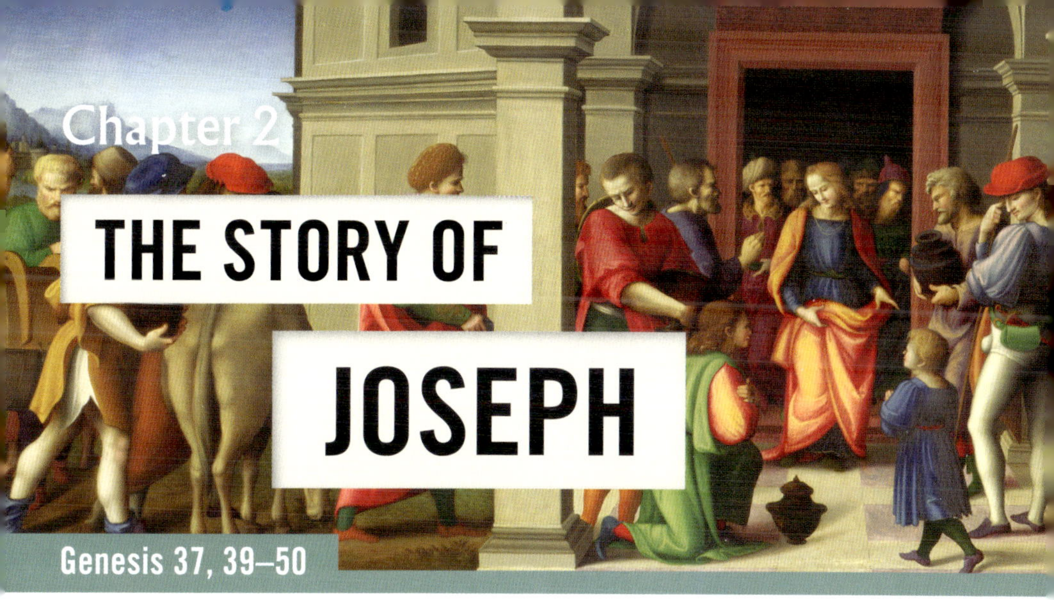

Chapter 2

THE STORY OF JOSEPH

Genesis 37, 39–50

THE STORY OF Joseph—an account of virtue, betrayal, and forgiveness—is the last of the stories of the patriarchs recorded in Genesis. Scholars and literary critics are fond of labeling the story a novella, a realistic story structured around a single line of suspense resolved by a rational, though unexpected, turning point in the action. This label is helpful, even though it is a bit anachronistic (the novella as a literary type usually applies to a style of short story that began to develop only during the Italian Renaissance). What is important to keep in mind is that the Joseph story is not a stand-alone account. Rather, it has many points of contact with the rest of the book of Genesis and the larger biblical narrative, as well as the cultural history of the ancient Near East. From this vantage point, we can see that it is also an explanation of how the descendants of Jacob—by now a man called Israel (Gen. 32:28)—come to live in Egypt, a place from which the exodus, the greatest story of redemption in the Old Testament, will unfold.

The story of Joseph focuses, as expected, on its main character, Joseph, but it is really a story of the family of Jacob: Joseph, his father (Jacob), and his eleven brothers. The women of the family are noticeably absent from the biblical account. Joseph is Jacob's favorite son even though he is the eleventh-oldest boy, not a natural formula for prominence in a patriarchy (playing favorites with one's children in any case rarely ends well). What Joseph does have going for him is that he is the oldest child of

Jacob's long-barren yet favorite wife, Rachel, making him the youngster on whom an aging father indulges. Joseph's name means "may the LORD add to me another son," the prayer of Rachel for enough sons to ensure her own well-being in an otherwise rough patriarchal world (Gen. 30:22–24). Rachel died in childbirth to her second son, Benjamin, well before the opening scene of the Joseph story (Gen. 35:16–19). This family tragedy surely fuels the angst that Jacob must feel as the subsequent events of the Joseph story unfold.

By the time the story of Joseph ends, all twelve sons are well on their way to becoming the ancestral heads of the tribes of Israel. This prompts us to read the narrative not just as a glimpse at individuals within a large and rather dysfunctional family but also in a way that anticipates a similar struggle for survival, self-preservation, and prominence that will come to characterize kingdom-building once everyone's descendants settle back in Canaan.

Scholars debate the date of the events described in Joseph's story, with the majority settling on the early Hyksos period (c. 1700–1550 BC). This was a time when ancient Egypt was divided into competing ruling dynasties. The pharaoh governing the eastern Nile delta, the part of Egypt in which most of the action of the Joseph story takes place, was of Semitic (likely Canaanite) origin. Early Jewish and Christian traditions nearly unanimously agree that the story of Joseph in Genesis was written much later by Moses (whether Moses lived in the fifteenth or the thirteenth centuries BC is also a matter of debate, with the latter now the majority view).

What's curious about the Joseph account is that Egypt is portrayed in a rather positive light. This is perhaps unexpected, given the more dominant theme in the Old Testament in which Egypt oppresses an enslaved Israel. We cannot be sure what would have prompted this favorable portrayal, other than it is an accurate account of what actually happened. But for sure, it is consistent with how much of the ancient world pictured Egypt most of the time: a place of nearly unlimited, renewable resources; an economic superpower where people could get ahead in life; a fascinating fulcrum of energy, culture, and art; but at the same time, an arena of potential danger for foreigners who try to get a bit too familiar with the place. This feeling seems to have been popular in Israel during the time of King Solomon, who married Pharaoh's daughter and nearly became more powerful in his lifetime than Pharaoh himself (1 Kings 9:15–19; 10:14–29). But throughout their long history of interactions with Egypt, the Israelites knew that that land wasn't their home. Theirs instead was a place in Canaan given to Abraham, Isaac, and Jacob, a marginal land that hones fidelity and trust in a God who promises most of all to care (Deut. 11:10–12).

The Travels of Joseph and His Brothers

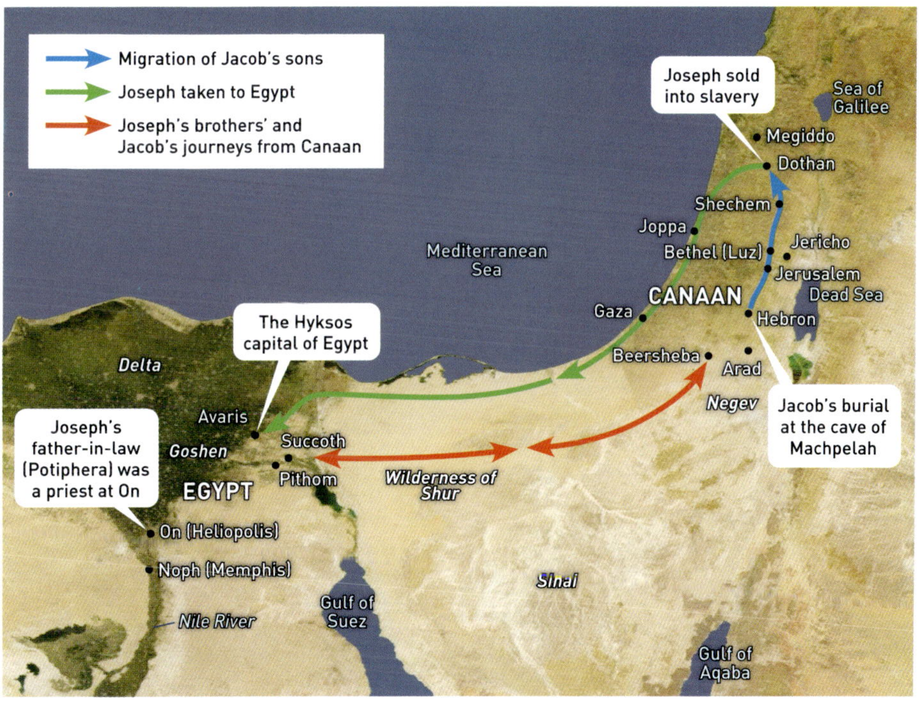

Themes in the Story of Joseph

The sovereignty and silence of God

God is sovereign. He decides what abilities, personalities, and tendencies people are born with, and he impacts how these play out during the course of their lives. This prompts us to wonder why Joseph has it all: the oldest son of Jacob's favorite wife; the handsome, capable one; the virtuous born leader; the one who prospers in spite of tremendous hardship; and the one who also comes to save the most powerful nation on earth from famine. Reminders of God's sovereignty on behalf of Joseph, his family, and even idolatrous Egypt appear at key intervals throughout the story (Gen. 39:2–6, 21–23; 41:38–40, 51–52; 45:4–9; 50:20). The blessings to which Joseph is born are also the cause of so much trouble as his life unfolds. But what his brothers (and others) mean for evil, God means for good (Gen. 50:20). Indeed, the brothers' plans to curtail Joseph's dreams of dominance end up being the very thing that begins the process by which he not only rules over them but also preserves everyone's lives in the end (Gen. 37:20; 45:5–11). The story of Joseph is reminiscent of the stories of Daniel and Esther, which also relate how a wise and virtuous hero who remains faithful to God rises to a high position in the royal court of a pagan foreign country.

God's hand of intervention is mentioned at key moments in the Joseph story, but not at every turn. Poor Joseph languishes in pits and prisons too often! We notice the silence of God in many other stories of the Bible as well. Faced with apparent divine inattention in similar circumstances, the human tendency is to question God's interest, ability, or power to intervene. Later biblical writers plead to God for insight and help (Pss. 39:12; 88:1–18), then speak of the need to wait, trust, and give praise in every circumstance (Ps. 40:1; Prov. 3:5–6; Phil. 4:11–13; Heb. 13:15). Other early writers commenting on the Joseph story tended to do the same. For instance, the apocryphal book *Testaments of the Twelve Patriarchs*, written in the second century BC, provides a succinct summary of what may well have been Joseph's own thoughts on the matter: "In all these things [God] takes his stand, and in various ways he offers assistance, even though for a brief time he may stand aside in order to test the disposition of the soul."[1]

The sovereignty of God is also seen in the choice of the younger over the older, a theme found throughout the book of Genesis (Abel over Cain, Isaac over Ishmael, Jacob over Esau, Joseph over Judah, Ephraim over Manasseh) and in other parts of the Bible (David over his brothers; cf. 1 Cor. 1:26). But in Joseph's story there's a twist: Judah, the fourth son of Leah (her youngest from natural conception), and Joseph, the oldest son of Rachel (yet the eleventh-born of Jacob) vie in the mind of the reader for prominence throughout the flow of the story. In the end, both receive favored blessings from Jacob, a setup for their subsequent competitive tribal histories in the land of Israel (Gen. 49:8–12, 22–26).

The human struggle for supremacy and self-preservation

Ambition, long-held grudges, jealousies, the lure of self-preservation, and self-elevation are all on display in the Joseph story, reflecting the natural tendencies of the human heart. The actions and attitudes of Joseph's brothers bring to a climax the same kinds of behaviors that their father Jacob exhibited with his twin Esau and with his uncle Laban earlier in the book of Genesis, and also the cavalier treatment by Abraham and Isaac of their wives (Gen. 12:10–20; 20:1–18; 26:6–11).

Although scholars tend to relish in the apparent sauciness of a young, fancy-coated Joseph, the biblical narrator is clear that in contrast to his brothers, Joseph's motives and actions are honorable throughout the story. We see this in Joseph's interactions with Potiphar's wife, by his instructions to the Egyptian officials to feed his brothers and care for his father, and by forgiving his brothers with the confession, "Am I in the place of God?" (Gen. 50:19). Even when he has the world's best chance at payback, Joseph chooses to orchestrate events so that his brothers are forgiven, aided, and honored, but also so they come to terms with the consequences of their sin.

Promise, blessing, and fulfillment

God's promise that Abraham's descendants will be a great nation in their own land might seem to be fulfilled when Jacob (renamed Israel) returns from Haran with his large family to settle in Canaan (Gen. 12:1–3; 33:18–20; 37:1). Yet just as a famine had prompted Abraham to move to Egypt, so it does for Jacob and his sons (Gen. 12:10; 41:53–57; 47:1). The Joseph story closes with the fulfillment of God's promises to the patriarchs only anticipated; we need to continue reading, starting with the book of Exodus, to complete the story.

Blessings in the Bible always flow from the context of a relationship that has been established between two parties (curses, on the other hand, signal a breakdown of that relationship). When God blesses someone, he intervenes in their life to do good things. When people bless other people, they also bestow favor. In the Bible, blessings spoken by a parent to a child often carry legal weight in that they transfer goods or authority to the next generation. This gives the one receiving the blessing a position of dominance over others, including siblings who do not receive the same spoken blessing. In every case, a blessing in the Bible is not well-wishing but is considered to hold real power affecting the circumstances of the recipient. God's promise of blessing to Abraham, Isaac, and Jacob (Gen. 12:2; 26:24; 28:13–15; 46:2–4) is inherited by all of Jacob's sons, though in various ways (Gen. 49:1–28; Deut. 33:1–29).

Events in the Story of Joseph

The Favored Son GENESIS 37:1–11

The young Joseph, extravagantly favored by his father, dreams twice. His first dream reveals that his brothers will be subservient to him, and the second indicates that his father will also bow before him.

When the story opens, Joseph is seventeen years old, normally an age of responsible adulthood in the ancient world. But for Joseph, this is a year of green confidence reinforced by an indulgent father. Earlier in Genesis, we learn that Joseph's older brothers are all half-brothers, sons of different mothers, reinforcing the consequences of their father's preferential treatment and their envy of their little brother (Gen. 29:31–30.24, 37:2). The tone of the story is set in the opening scene by the "bad report" that Joseph brings to Jacob about his brothers (Gen. 37:2). While left to wonder about its content and justification, we are prompted to ask, "What good can come from this? How is this going to work?" From the opening scene the human condition is on raw display.

Jacob endows Joseph with "a robe of many colors" (Gen. 37:3). The Hebrew term *kutonet passim* literally means "tunic of palms," the palm being the inner, flat part of a hand, not a kind of tree. This name has led to a variety of suggestions about the style and pattern of Joseph's coat:

- One likely idea is that it is garment with long sleeves reaching to the hands. This is the case of the robe of Tamar, sister of Absalom, the only other garment in the Bible called a *kutonet passim* (2 Sam. 13:18–19).
- A second idea, suggested in a Jewish commentary on Genesis written around AD 400, is that this is a garment so light and delicate that it can be folded into one's palm.[2]
- The most popular suggestion, following the Greek translation of the story in the Septuagint (third century BC), is that this is a coat of many colors, apparently decorated with variegated hand-size pieces. (The essayist Francine Prose described the favorite page in her childhood coloring book as depicting Joseph wearing a "coat with rich opportunities for every crayon in the box."[3]) Supporting this interpretation, a painting found in tomb at Beni-hasan, Egypt, dating to the nineteenth century BC, roughly the time of the patriarchs, depicts Canaanites immigrating to Egypt wearing sleeveless clothing decorated with bright colors.

Whatever Joseph's robe looked like, the word *extravagant* applies in all cases.

As if his special garment and his bad report weren't already enough to anger his brothers, young Joseph receives two divine dreams; in both dreams, all his brothers bow down to him! In the ancient world, dreams were generally thought to reveal future events. Temple and palace officials had, among their personnel, wise men and diviners whose responsibility it was to determine the meanings of dreams. In this light, it is significant that Joseph's family needs no intermediary to correctly interpret Joseph's two dreams. Later, some of the kings of Judah will practice divination and other forms of spiritism in an attempt to know and control the future, and they are roundly condemned by the prophets for doing so (e.g., Deut. 18:9–11; 2 Kings 17:17; 2 Chron. 33:6; Jer. 14:13–14; Ezek. 12:24; cf. Ezek. 21:18–23).

Joseph's "Death" GENESIS 37:12–36

After looking for his brothers in Shechem, Joseph finds them in Dothan where they sell him to a passing caravan of Ishmaelites (also called Midianites).

Shechem and Dothan were thriving Canaanite cities at the time of the Joseph story. That the brothers, based in Hebron 40 to 50 miles (65 to 80 km) to the south, are able to graze their flocks within the economic zone of these cities implies that they already had gained the right to do so. It was a common practice in the ancient Near East for shepherds to establish grazing and trading rights within the resource base of urban centers to strengthen their own positions and provide a local hedge against famine. We might assume that Abraham and Jacob had already secured these rights for themselves and their descendants during their prior journeys to Shechem (Gen. 12:6–7; 33:18–20).

By mutual consent, Joseph's brothers initially plan to kill him as soon as he arrives in Dothan. They agree to throw him into a pit, probably a large, rounded underground cistern from which he can't climb out, apparently intending to leave him to the elements until he dies of starvation. But as Jacob's first-born, Reuben plans to save Joseph's life by pulling him out later. Reuben's actions are what we should expect, given the responsibility of the eldest male in a patriarchal society to protect and provide for members of his family. But unbeknownst to Reuben, Judah suggests that rather than abandoning Joseph, they sell him to a passing caravan. Judah's motives are ambiguous at best and raw deceit at worst. His words say, "Let not our hand be upon him, for he is our brother, our own flesh" (Gen. 37:27), but his thoughts appear to be quite different: "Let's rid ourselves of Joseph forever and profit financially in the process." In the end, the brothers' plot—and God's plans—are forwarded by Judah, O-man-of-unclean-heart, from whom rulership over Israel eventually will come (cf. Gen. 49:8–10).

A cistern opening typical of those found throughout the hills of ancient Canaan

In a clipped note that links the episode of Joseph thrown into a pit with the arrival of the camel caravan we read, "Then they sat down to eat" (Gen. 37:25). Whenever people share a meal in the Bible, it is nearly always to celebrate an occasion or enjoy what we have come to call "table fellowship," a barriers-down, genuine acceptance of each other. The note that the brothers "sat down to eat" in the midst of what they have just done, and are about to do, though tense, is as loud a cry of wrongdoing as any in the book of Genesis.

The brothers sell Joseph to traveling merchants who are identified in the text as both Ishmaelite and Midianite (Gen. 37:25, 27–28, 36). *Ishmaelite* is probably the more general term and *Midianite* references the specific people group. The Midianite homeland was east of the Gulf of Aqaba/Gulf of Eilat, the northeastern arm of the Red Sea. The caravan seems to be tracking the spice route out of the southern Arabian Peninsula, picking up commodities and trading with local populations as they go. From the hills of Gilead east of the Jordan River they bend west, passing by Dothan on the most convenient cut-through that joins up with the coastal route to Egypt. They are carrying exotic goods (gum, balm, and myrrh), spices of medicinal and ritual value. The Midianite traders are forerunners of a host of later caravanners who commanded rich profit from the Arabian Spice Route, including the Nabateans at the time of the New Testament.

Apparently these traveling merchants see an opportunity to engage in trading humans as well. They purchase Joseph for twenty pieces of silver (Gen. 37:28). This was the going price for a slave in the early to mid-second millennium BC. Texts from Egypt's thirteenth dynasty (c. 1800–1650 BC) indicate that it was not unusual for Semites from the region of Canaan or Arabia to be servants in Egypt, and some were given responsibilities of trust by their owners.

Joseph's bad report to Jacob about his brothers started the sequence (Gen. 37:2). Now the brothers scheme to tell their father that a fierce animal has eaten Joseph (Gen. 37:20, 33). The words *bad* and *fierce* are the same Hebrew word, *ra'ah*, an indication in the story that what goes around comes around, even for our poor Joseph. The same Hebrew word is used again at the very end of the Joseph story, this time from the mouth

Children of Jacob Sell their Brother Joseph (Konstantin Flavitsky, 1855)

of Joseph himself: What his brothers intended for evil (*ra'ah*), God meant for good (Gen. 50:20).

We must pause in disbelief as we read how the brothers tell their father the worst sort of lie imaginable, one that strikes at the root of everything they and their culture—and the heart of God—hold dear. Fratricide, horrible as it is, is one thing; destroying their father's future is unconscionable. And to salve the wound by comforting Jacob with the poison of an ongoing lie is sheer betrayal and an insidious, self-preserving deceit. The glue that holds life together is undone. Joseph, for all practical purposes, is dead (he may even have the same feelings about himself). But he certainly isn't forgotten, not by daddy nor by his guilty brothers, who somehow manage for nearly twenty years to keep a straight face in the presence of their grieving father.

YOM KIPPUR

The apocryphal book *Jubilees*, dating to the second century BC, claims that Jacob heard of Joseph's supposed death on the tenth day of the seventh month, the same day of the year that Moses would decree that Israel observe the Day of Atonement, Yom Kippur (Lev. 16:29–34). On Yom Kippur, Jews (descendants of Jacob) would sacrifice a goat—the same kind of animal that Joseph's brothers killed to stain his coat and deceive their father—as an offering to cover their sins of the previous year. *Jubilees* decrees that the children of Israel are to do this every year "because they [that is, as Judah] caused the affection of their father to grieve for Joseph."[4]

Joseph in Potiphar's House GENESIS 39:1–23

Joseph is sold to Potiphar, the captain of Pharaoh's guard, where he prospers even in the face of false accusations by Potiphar's wife that land him in prison.

Because Pharaoh is not mentioned by name either here in Joseph's story or in the stories of Abraham or Moses, we are not able to date of any of the events of these stories with precision (cf. Gen. 12:15; Ex. 1:11; 5:1). The first pharaoh that the Bible mentions by name is Shishak, who invaded Israel in the fifth year of King Rehoboam, son of Solomon (1 Kings 14:25).

Potiphar is a version of a known Egyptian name meaning "he whom Ra [the sun god] has given" (cf. Gen. 41:45). This particular Potiphar is not otherwise attested in Egyptian texts. His position as captain of the guard is likely a military role, indicating that he, and hence Joseph, probably live in the capital city of Egypt, in close vicinity to Pharaoh's palace and the royal administration (Gen. 37:36; 39:1). The name of this city is also not mentioned in the story.

Ra, depicted as a falcon-headed man carrying the sun on his head

In Hebrew, the word for both slave and servant is the same: *'ebed*. (This will have parallels to, and important implications for, how we might understand the status of the Israelites in Egypt at the time of Moses.) Slaves or servants, even if purchased, were tied to their owners on a relationship basis that gave them certain rights of their own. The nature of this relationship was not static. The owner, or master, could strengthen, or lessen, the responsibilities and obligations of the servant based on his or her skills and abilities. Joseph is Potiphar's personal servant, living in the same housing compound and in charge of Potiphar's household and assets.

While in the house of Potiphar, "the LORD was with Joseph, and he became a successful man" (Gen. 39:2). Joseph prospers in all that he does, but we should not think of his prosperity only, or even primarily, in terms of economy. As the psalmist declares, "Blessed is the man … [whose] delight is in the law of the LORD.… He is like a tree planted by streams of water that yields its fruit in its season, and its leaf does not wither. In all that he does, he prospers" (Ps. 1:1–3). Joseph is successful in whatever situation he finds himself, not only under Potiphar but also later in prison (Gen. 39:21–23) and then in Pharaoh's court (Gen. 41:37–45). God sees something in Joseph that even his own family doesn't.

Egyptians and their neighbors, depicted in the tomb of Pharaoh Seti I, Valley of the Kings

Joseph is described as "handsome in form and appearance," attracting the attention of Potiphar's wife (Gen. 39:6). The Egyptians also had noticed that his great-grandmother, Sarah, was very beautiful (Gen. 12:14). We know from ancient Egyptian art that the Egyptians portrayed idealized rather than realistic body types (as does ancient Greek art) and carefully distinguished the physical appearance of Egyptians from their non-Egyptian neighbors. Israelite readers of the stories of Joseph and Sarah must have relished in the description of their ancestors being attractive to their well-heeled neighbors.

Joseph's refusal to bow to the sexual advances of Potiphar's wife (who, like Pharaoh, remains forever nameless), even if it means that he will lose his status and be cast into prison, is pure and unambiguous. In this, he stands in stark moral contrast to his brothers, especially Judah (cf. Gen. 38:1–26). Earlier, Joseph's brothers had stripped him of his fancy garment, removing the sign of his favored status and leaving him open and vulnerable to the forces of nature. Now, Joseph intentionally leaves his garment in the grip of Potiphar's wife to flee from her, a visible indication (and symbolic foreshadowing) that he is about to exchange his favored status for the vulnerable squalor of an Egyptian prison.

Joseph in the Pit—Again GENESIS 40:1–41:52

While in prison, Joseph interprets the dreams of two fellow prisoners. He is released two years later when he interprets Pharaoh's dreams predicting seven years of plenty followed

by seven years of famine. Pharaoh responds by elevating Joseph to a high position in Egypt.

At the start of Joseph's story it's his dreams that get him thrown into a pit, and at this part of the narrative it's the divine dreams of others—the cupbearer and the baker—that get him out of the pit of prison. Samples of dreams and their interpretation are common in Dream Book texts from ancient Egypt and Mesopotamia. They were part of a long tradition of divination which attempted to use or manipulate elements of this world to predict the future (e.g., 1 Kings 22:9–12; Isa. 3:3; Ezek. 21:21; Dan. 1:20). In the Bible, dreams as a means of prediction occur primarily with the patriarchs, in the time of the exile (Dan. 1–7), and with the birth of Jesus (Matt. 1:20; 2:12–22). The Bible condemns all manner of fortune-telling, although it does recognize the validity of dreams when the giver of interpretations is God. The content of the dreams in the Joseph story are related in fine detail, with enough specifics that the reader knows it is not possible to interpret all of them exactly right. This confirms Pharaoh's words that Joseph must be someone "in whom is the Spirit of God" (Gen. 41:38) since the interpretations of dreams "belong to God" (Gen. 40:8).

Pharaoh admits Joseph has discernment and wisdom that others in Egypt don't possess (Gen. 41:39). This is a momentous admission since Egypt has a well-established tradition of wisdom, recognized across the

THE CUPBEARER

The chief cupbearer is a king's personal attendant who serves drinks at the royal table, but his responsibilities to care for the king's welfare and safety are certainly broader (cf. Neh. 1:11–2:1). The king must trust him implicitly.

In Joseph's story, both the cupbearer and the baker are called *saris* in Hebrew, a term corresponding to a known rank of dignitaries and officials in the Egyptian administration.

ancient Near East (cf. 1 Kings 4:30). By the end of his story, Joseph shows that he is also a more able administrator than Pharaoh (Gen. 41:37–44; 47:13–26).

The position to which Pharaoh elevates Joseph may have been Grand Vizier, called "Overseer of Royal Estates" in Egyptian documents; or it is possible that he is appointed to a more specific task, also directly under Pharaoh, something like a vice president of agriculture and famine relief, in modern terminology. Why would Pharaoh elevate a non-Egyptian to such an important position? Egyptians typically held foreigners, even those living in Egypt, at a suspicious arm's length and allowed them to remain only if they served larger Egyptian purposes: to be assigned to units in the army, for example, or to act as servants, or to perform menial labor. The most plausible exception to this pattern is that Pharaoh himself is a foreigner, as was the case during the Egyptian fifteenth (Hyksos) dynasty (c. 1650–1550 BC). Canaanites and other Semites had been infiltrating Egypt for centuries prior to the founding of the Hyksos dynasty. Eventually they gained enough demographic strength to establish their own rule in the eastern Nile delta with their head, a Semite, as the pharaoh. The Hyksos base of operation was Avaris (Tell ed-Dab'a), adjacent to the land of Goshen where Joseph and his family came to live (Gen. 45:10). Many scholars find this context a comfortable fit for a pharaoh who would allow a non-Egyptian Semite to gain a prominent position in the land and openly invite his family to join him. Other scholars instead place Moses's elevation in Pharaoh's household under the Hyksos dynasty, pushing Joseph back into Egypt's Middle Kingdom (c. 1950–1650 BC), which was ruled from Upper (southern) Egypt and only by native Egyptians.

Hyksos juglet decorated with incised dots forming geometric patterns

The Greek historian Herodotus called Egypt "an acquired country, the gift of the Nile."[5] Egypt was dependent on the Nile, which prior to the construction of the Aswan Low Dam in 1902 flooded every year from mid-summer through autumn. This annual inundation brought a fresh layer of enriched soil with it. The amount of the submergence—and hence the fertility of the upcoming growing season—was in turn dependent on the prior late-winter and spring rainfall in Ethiopia and the great lakes region of East Africa. In the Egyptian pantheon, Hapy was the god of the Nile inundation, a deity who in effect controlled the economy of Egypt since water, the very life of its people, was subject to his will. Years of sufficient flooding followed by years of not enough flooding were fairly common in ancient Egypt but couldn't be predicted and hence the people prepared for that only in general ways. Joseph, in the biblical story, is preparing Egypt in specific ways with divine insight into what's to come. Though he certainly doesn't invent the idea of storing grain in storehouses nor of imposing taxes on the harvest, his prompt to Pharaoh that this should be done *now* is certainly appropriate (Gen. 41:34–36).

A dual depiction of Hapy uniting Upper and Lower Egypt with the river

Joseph is given the Egyptian name Zaphenath-paneah (perhaps "the god speaks and he [Joseph] lives"). He then marries Asenath ("she belongs to [the creator goddess] Neith"), daughter of Potiphera, priest of On (Gen. 41:45). The city of On was dedicated to the sun god Amun-Ra, head of the Egyptian pantheon; its ruins are in modern Heliopolis, "Sun City," in the northern part of metropolitan Cairo. The priest of On was one of the most powerful men in ancient Egypt, in some ways a rival to Pharaoh himself.

Throughout the Genesis account, Joseph is portrayed as a person of the highest moral character, the only one in Genesis described as possessing the Spirit of God—and that from the mouth of Pharaoh! (Gen. 41:38). But what is Joseph doing here? Is he assimilating into Egyptian culture and worldview by marrying Asenath, or is he just being a good guest in the country? What is he, a God-fearing Israelite, thinking by taking the reins of this foreign country?

We are far enough along in the Joseph story to realize that the story is ripe with questions that have no answers. Why didn't Joseph tell his Midianite body snatchers to detour to Hebron on their way to Egypt so that his father could ransom him back? Once in Egypt, why didn't he run from Potiphar, blend into other groups of Semites in Goshen, and make his way back home the first chance he gets, hoping that his brothers will have gotten over it by then? (Never does the narrator say, "God told Joseph to stay put.") Or, once Joseph had command second to Pharaoh in Egypt, why didn't he send word back to his family to let them know he's alive and well, or at least find out if they're okay? The distance from Goshen to Canaan isn't that far, and traders and Egyptian officials head back and forth on a regular basis all the time. Eventually, we will read that Joseph realizes that his being in Egypt is part of God's plan to save his family from famine, but there is no indication that he knows this until quite late in the story. We can say, "God kept him there," but how aware might he be of that in the meantime? For sure, life was more comfortable in Egypt than back in Canaan, and once he marries, he has personal ties to keep him put. God's big-picture plan is for Jacob's family to immigrate to Egypt, grow and multiply, and then return to Canaan through the hand of Moses; but we only know this from later stories. Even so, God never explicitly tells Joseph's father to immigrate to Egypt, but rather just "do not be afraid" for "I myself will go down with you" (Gen. 46:3–4). Perhaps we do Joseph a disservice in his own story if we fail to ask what seem like normal what-were-you-thinking questions as the story unfolds.

Joseph in the Palace GENESIS 41:53–42:38

During a severe famine in Canaan, Joseph's brothers travel to Egypt to buy grain. Joseph hides his identity from them, gives them grain at no cost, and bids them return to Canaan, so they can bring his younger brother,

Benjamin, back with them next time. Joseph holds Simeon hostage until they return.

Because of the fertility of the Nile delta, Egypt was the major grain supplier for the ancient Mediterranean world (cf. Gen. 41:54, 57). This role fueled Egypt's periodic rise as an empire. The phrase "all the earth came to Egypt to Joseph to buy grain, because the famine was severe over all the earth" is speaking of the region of the world that is in relatively close proximity to Egypt and would normally rely on Egypt for trade (Gen. 41:57).

The effects of famine are strongest in Egypt and Canaan (Gen. 47:13). This famine is particularly severe because the weather patterns prompting it persist for several years (Gen. 43:1–2). Both Egypt, which depends on the Nile, and Canaan, where water falls as seasonal rain, are bounded by desert climates that can easily overwhelm the land in a year of water shortages. Most people tended to live hand to mouth even in the better years, with adequate harvests never a sure thing and the slow grip of starvation an ever-present reality. Prolonged famines eventually affected all aspects of life, prompting inflation, theft, disease, even cannibalism (cf. Lam. 4:9–10); and unsettled masses were quick to blame anyone in authority (the gods included) for their misfortune. A text from Egypt's First Intermediate Period (Dynasties 7–10, c. 2160–2055 BC) summarized it this way: "The whole country has become like locusts going upstream and downstream [in search of food]."[6] Joseph's initiatives to store grain and then buy land to centralize grain production is consistent with various initiatives in ancient Egypt over the millennia to mitigate against famine (Gen. 41:53–57; 47:13–26).

This field-lined canal provides a timeless view of life along the Nile.

Joseph's brothers arrive in Egypt to purchase grain. More than twenty years have passed since they sold him into slavery (Gen. 37:2; 41:46–48). Joseph quickly accuses his inquiring brothers of wanting "to see the nakedness of the land," that is, to see if the land lies unprotected, vulnerable, and open to invasion (Gen. 42:9; cf. 42:12). This was a real issue for ancient Egypt. As the Mediterranean world's chief supplier of grain, the country faced the constant threat of foreigners wanting to infiltrate, settle, and make use of the land for themselves. The eastern Nile delta (land of Goshen) especially was an open sieve in spite of attempts at various times in Egyptian history to guard its frontier with walled forts. Shepherds from the Sinai, the Arabian Peninsula, and Canaan—all looking for new grazing lands or, worse yet, places to settle down—were especially troublesome for the Egyptians who needed to protect their crops from hungry teeth not their own. Egyptians preferred to graze cattle, and those in the eastern delta would compete with foreign shepherds (herders of sheep and goats) for foraging resources (this undoubtedly lay behind the Egyptian dislike of shepherds as confirmed in Genesis 46:34).

In their father's absence, Reuben, the oldest brother, is the one who holds authority over the others and so has the ability to sway their attitude in whatever situation might arise (Gen. 42:22; cf. Gen. 37:21–22). He and his brothers recognize that their troubles in securing grain in Egypt are somehow due to their treatment of Joseph years before, but they don't recognize that this is the same man with whom they are now speaking. Their guilt is palpable, still fresh, over two decades after their horrendous

Grain harvesting in ancient Egypt, from the tomb of Menna (12th century BC), an Egyptian official who bore the tile "Overseer of Fields and Lord of the Two Lands"

offense to their brother, their father, and God. Why else would they feel the need to tell this Egyptian official that one of them "is no more," then blame each other for what must be the cause of their current troubles (Gen. 42:13, 21–22)? We can imagine that for an agonizingly long period of time they have been looking over their collective shoulders, a years-long gnawing haunted by what surely, someday, must bring the vengeance of God (Gen. 42:21; 44:20, 27–29). In a delightful "uh-oh!" the narrator tells us that Joseph, like us, already knows (Gen. 42:23).

We would like Joseph to act with virtue throughout this one-sided negotiation, but when it gets down to hitting in the weeds, perhaps we should allow him some true emotion. What is he doing? Is it revenge? Is it to rub his brothers' noses in the fulfillment of his dreams? To get them to fess up to their prior actions? Certainly it isn't good-natured kidding. That Joseph sends their brothers back home with instructions to fetch Benjamin—his only full brother and their father's now-favorite—and returns their purchase money for grain unawares indicate that he has a long-term scheme in mind. Joseph also knows that Reuben must be the one who tells Jacob that innocent Benjamin is wanted in Egypt. So it is Simeon, the second oldest and next in line in terms of patriarchal value, who is the necessary choice to remain as hostage (Gen. 42:24). The brothers must wonder how this Egyptian ruler knows that Simeon is the proper next man up.

Joseph's Big Reveal GENESIS 43:1–45:15

With Benjamin in tow, the brothers return to Egypt to purchase more grain. After pretending to frame Benjamin for theft of his silver cup, Joseph reveals himself to them.

Judah steps up to take full responsibility for Benjamin's safety when they return to Egypt (Gen. 43:3–10). Unlike the earlier episode when he instigated the sale of Joseph to the Midianite traders with clearly questionable motives, Judah now is genuinely concerned about Joseph's only full-brother and his father. This is a welcome foreshadowing of the leadership role that the tribe of Judah will play once everyone's descendants are back in the land of Israel.

Genesis 43:11 provides a delicious detail in the story: a list of foods and spices that Jacob has his sons carry back to Joseph in Egypt (balm, honey, spices, myrrh, pistachios, and almonds). The list is more elaborate than the commodities that the Midianite camel caravan had taken to Egypt with Joseph in tow, though of lesser quantities (Gen. 37:25). Later texts provide a list of staple foods typical to the land of Canaan (Deut. 8:7–8), but the products sent by Jacob are the very best the land has to offer.

Almonds and pistachios

We can sympathize with the brothers' apprehension in returning to Egypt, even though we, as readers, have privileged information that everything will be all right (Gen. 43:15–18). What we don't know yet is exactly how it will all turn out.

The sumptuous banquet hosted by Joseph is particularly suspenseful (Gen. 43:26–34). Because sharing a meal carries connotations of acceptance, the text makes sure we know that Egyptians and foreigners typically don't eat together. The brothers must expect to be reduced to servants, imprisoned, or worse yet, treated to a banquet, seated according to age (how would this Egyptian know who is older than whom?), and asked personal questions as if Pharaoh's second-in-command actually cares about them. That the brothers are amazed is putting things mildly (Gen. 43:33). The last time the Joseph story included an episode of the brothers sharing a meal was when they were in the process of getting rid of Joseph back in Dothan, nonchalant to his fate or their father's response (Gen. 37:25). Joseph's feast is, in stark contrast, redemptive.

We're informed in Genesis 44:5 that Joseph has a silver cup for "divination." Even though divination is forbidden by later biblical writers, at this stage of biblical revelation we must grant Joseph the leniency to participate in certain aspects of Egyptian life—or at least claim to do so (Gen. 44:15). Jewish historian Josephus cleans up the story for first-century-AD sensibilities by simply calling the vessel Joseph's "own favorite silver drinking cup."[7]

When Joseph places his silver cup in Benjamin's grain sack, the scene is set to reveal his true motives all along: he wants his brothers to own their original sin. Joseph tells his steward to confront the brothers with the line, "Why have you repaid evil [*ra'ah*] for good?" (Gen. 44:4). This is a tight twist of the screw, a climactic "Now I've gotcha!" as the brothers are lulled into believing they are home free. Yet the encounter serves to anticipate an even greater climax later: Joseph's full forgiveness in reassuring them that "you meant evil [*ra'ah*] against me, but God meant it for good" (Gen. 50:20). Incredulous as to their presumed guilt, the brothers vow that if the cup is found in one of their sacks, the one with the hot goods will die and the rest will all be slaves. The vow is rash but to the point. When the silver cup is found in Benjamin's sack, they admit their guilt, but Joseph turns the screw even tighter: Only Benjamin will to be sold into slavery—Joseph knowing full well that they remember that they had done the same to him (Gen. 44:6–17). It is Judah who steps up by offering to take Benjamin's place in prison, faithful to the vow he had made to Jacob. Throughout, the

The Finding of Joseph's Cup in Benjamin's Sack (Nicolas de Poilly, 1698)

brothers never do admit to this Egyptian lord that they are responsible for Joseph's demise, but their sincere regret that their current troubles will kill their father with grief is confession enough for Joseph. That Joseph's brothers finally own up to their guilt is proven by their deeds.

For Joseph, it is now time to reveal his true identity to his brothers. He does so with great emotion, having dismissed his attendants from the room so that the moment will have all the privacy it deserves. Joseph's brothers are "dismayed" (Gen. 45:3); we can perhaps think of a number of other words as well, "shocked" being the least of them. We can also imagine them frozen in position as Joseph gives a long explanation of what has transpired over the last twenty years, and why ("It was not you who sent me here, but God.... God has made me lord of all Egypt"; Gen. 45:8–9). Like the capable administrator he now is, Joseph reveals his plans to have his entire extended family join him in Egypt. His brothers finally weep and only then are able to speak.

Joseph's Family in Egypt GENESIS 45:16–47:31; 50:1–26

Jacob and his family move to Egypt where they prosper, and Jacob eventually dies. Joseph also dies, but not before he forgives his brothers.

Pharaoh invites Jacob and his family to move to "the best of the land of Egypt" (Gen. 45:18; cf. 45:20; 47:11). The Hebrew term is *tov eretz*, "the good of the land." This phrase takes us two directions: back to Eden, which is the first place in the Bible called "good" (Gen. 1:12, 18, 21, 25, 31), and forward to what will become the land of Israel, also described as "a good land" (Deut. 8:7). On the one hand, the move to Egypt is a pre-fulfillment of the promise of blessing to the descendants of Abraham, welcome because of the difficulty of having to make a go of it in Canaan where recovery from famine is not so easy (Gen. 46:3; 47:27). On the other hand, this invitation should be subsumed to the larger theme that Egypt, however good it may be in terms of sustaining life, is not to be Israel's permanent home. While the promise to Abraham detours Jacob and his sons to Egypt, they belong back in Canaan, the land of Israel (Gen. 12:7; 15:13–16; Deut. 11:10–12).

As he leaves Canaan for Egypt, Jacob passes through Beersheba in the arid Negev desert (Gen. 46:1). It is likely that during the famine, he had been grazing his flocks in the higher, hilly regions around Hebron where the scant rainfall still produced sufficient grass (cf. Gen. 37:14). Abraham and Isaac both built altars in Beersheba and established it as the family's base of operations (Gen. 21:22–24; 26:23–31). When there, Jacob offers sacrifices and God appears to him in a night vision (Gen. 46:2–4), reminiscent of the night vision in which God promised his grandfather Abraham that even though his descendants would be servants for four hundred years "in a land that is not theirs," they will eventually return to their homeland in Canaan (Gen. 15:12–16). In Jacob's vision, God reaffirms the promises of protection, progeny, and land that he already had made to Abraham, Isaac, and Jacob (Gen. 46:3–4). In between these promises, which were given decades apart from each other, are long stretches of time during which God is largely silent and the patriarchs struggle to live in ways that are faithful to each other and to him.

The migration of Jacob's family and all their possessions to the land of Goshen in the eastern Nile delta mirrors large-scale migrations of Semites to the region throughout the second millennium BC. This is illustrated by the Beni-hasan tomb painting depicting Semites in colorful clothing coming to Egypt to live, with their goods packed on donkeys and their bows unstrung in peace.

Beni-hasan tomb painting, depicting Canaanites migrating to Egypt (19th century BC)

The list of Jacob's descendants totals seventy persons (Gen. 46:8–27; cf. Ex 1:5). Not coincidentally, this is also the number of nations listed in the so-called Table of Nations, the descendants of Noah who go out to repopulate the earth (Gen. 10:1–32). By implication, Jacob's descendants function as a new kind of humanity, focused on God's promises to Abraham, Isaac, and Jacob. A closing statement in the Pentateuch, Deuteronomy 32:8–9, declares that God "divided mankind ... according to the number of the sons of God [i.e., the Israelites]" but that God's own portion "is his people, Jacob his allotted heritage." As we might now expect, it is Judah, not Reuben, who takes the lead to guide everyone to Goshen (Gen. 46:28).

Due to the severity of the famine, Joseph arranges that additional land in Egypt be appropriated by the crown; that one-fifth of the grain crop produced in Egypt will be paid as tax to Pharaoh; but that land owned by the priests will remain under temple ownership (Gen. 47:13–26). That Joseph is successful in doing so attests to his great loyalty to Pharaoh, his skills in statesmanship, and the abject severity of the famine. While details about these transactions are elusive when we compare them to historical records in Egypt, Joseph's actions are consistent with the overall tendency in the second half of the second millennium BC to strengthen the land holdings of the crown and the temples. According to the Egyptian worldview, Pharaoh is the Egyptian deities' representative on earth and so owns all the land anyway, yet the actual practice of how much grain is to be paid in taxes varied from time to time.

Both Jacob and Joseph want their bones to be buried back in the land promised to Abraham rather than in Egypt (Gen. 47:29–31; 50:22–26). After Jacob dies, he is embalmed in the manner of Egyptian royalty. His body is then accompanied by a large royal entourage to the tomb of Abraham and Isaac at the cave in the field of Machpelah outside of Mamre near Hebron (Gen. 49:28–50:14). Similar parades accompanying royal marriages and burials are known from Egyptian records. As for Joseph, centuries later the Israelites carry his mummified bones with them when they leave Egypt during the exodus, burying them in Shechem where Jacob had once purchased land (Gen. 50:25–26; Ex. 13:19; Josh.

24:32; cf. Gen. 33:18–19; John 4:5–6). Both sites remain places of memory, pilgrimage, and worship for Jews, Christians, and Muslims today.

Like his grandfather Abraham, Jacob made a seasonal home in the arable grazing lands around the Canaanite city-state of Hebron.

Farewell Blessings GENESIS 48:1–49:33

As his last act, Jacob adopts the two sons of Joseph, Manasseh and Ephraim, and blesses them. He then blesses his twelve sons. Joseph and Judah are given preeminence in Jacob's blessings but in different ways.

Jacob blesses Joseph's younger son Ephraim as if he, rather than Manasseh, were the firstborn (Gen. 48:1–22). This parallels Isaac's blessing of Jacob over Esau and reflects a biblical theme of the younger (or weaker) person chosen over the older (or stronger). Jacob's blessing is that in Ephraim and Manasseh "let my name be carried on, and the name of my fathers Abraham and Isaac; and let them grow into a multitude in the midst of the earth" (Gen. 48:16). This gives Jacob's grandsons, born to Joseph and his Egyptian wife, Asenath, status equal to Jacob's other sons, setting the stage for their eventual preeminence as tribal entities in the land of Israel.

Jacob's blessings to Reuben, Simeon, and Levi (his oldest three sons) disqualify them for future preeminence (Gen. 49:2–7). This makes room for Judah, his fourth-born, whose character is radically transformed during the Joseph story, to receive a blessing focused on his eventual rulership over all of his brothers (Gen. 49:8–12). With it, the impact of the dreams of Joseph passes to Judah from which the line of David and the messianic scepter will come.

Great value was placed in the ancient world on having many descendants and in securing rights to live on profitable land. Jacob's blessing to Judah focuses on people, while his blessing to Joseph focuses on land. This will produce an ongoing tension between the Joseph tribes (Ephraim and Manasseh) on the one hand and the tribe of Judah on the other that we can track throughout the Old Testament. Which will be the most preeminent as Israel grows from a family to a tribal confederation to a kingdom? What will that tension look like as it unfolds in real time? Ephraim and Manasseh eventually become the heartland of the northern kingdom of Israel, governed by kings ruling from Samaria, while Judah will be the main tribal entity in the southern kingdom of Judah, centered on Jerusalem. According to 1 Chronicles 5:2, "Judah became strong among his brothers and a chief came from him" even though "the birthright belonged to Joseph." While a good deal of intrigue probably lies behind this summary statement, Psalm 78:67–68 places the choice of the line of David, descendant of Judah, squarely on the sovereignty of God: "He rejected the tent of Joseph . . . but chose the tribe of Judah, Mount Zion, which he loves."

TRIBAL BLESSINGS

The blessings that Jacob bestows on his twelve sons recall their past deeds (some were for good, some for ill) and speaks of their futures as individual tribes. Each blessing is aptly suited to the character of each particular son. All of the blessings are short, except for those bestowed upon Judah and Joseph (Gen. 49:1–27). Joseph's blessing, the richest in language of the twelve, focuses on the fertility of the land that his tribal descendants will receive (Gen. 49:22–26; cf. Deut. 33:13–17).

JOSEPH IN LATER WRITINGS

- Other than the Joseph story, the events of Joseph's life are mentioned in the Bible only in Psalm 105:16–22, on the lips of Stephen in Acts 7:9–18, and in Hebrews 11:21–22 among the list of faithful men of God.

- As the Jews suffered under foreign domination in the mid-second century BC, the father of the Maccabees, Mattathias, also spoke of Joseph as an inspiring example of someone who had kept God's commands under times of distress.[8]

- Rabbinic and early Christian writers chose to emphasize Joseph's virtue and morality as a model for behavior, especially in times of trial. A line in *Apostolic Constitutions*, a book of Christian liturgy dating to the second or third centuries AD, states that Joseph's elevation as ruler in Egypt was a reward of "the self-control that [God] enables."[9]

- Under the Roman Empire, a large population of Jews lived in Egypt where they came in constant contact with a thriving and seductive gentile world. Intermarriage and assimilation was a live issue, then as now, prompting an anonymous author to pen a long tale in Greek titled "Joseph and Aseneth." In this widely popular story composed sometime after the New Testament, Joseph prays to God for the idol-worshiping Asenath's conversion. After she destroys her idols and repents, an angel declares that Asenath will be the protector of any foreigner in Egypt who turns to God. Joseph then marries Asenath in a ceremony presided over by the pharaoh.

- In the fourth century AD, St. Ambrose, bishop of Milan, saw parallels between the life of Joseph and that of Jesus: both suffered and were sold, elevated, and forgiving.[10] These themes have inspired all manner of art and writings throughout Christian and later Western secular history, keeping the memory of Joseph alive, even though the details of his life are too often obscure.

Study Questions

1. Describe the characters of Joseph, Reuben, and Judah as they appear in the opening episode of the story (Gen. 37). What questions arise about their motives? Their attitudes? Their temperament? Who is the most righteous? Conflicted? Guilty?
2. How is the human struggle for supremacy and self-preservation apparent in the story of Joseph? Where is it most excusable—and where most egregious?
3. How does Joseph prove his character by his deeds once he is in Egypt?
4. Why do you think that Joseph doesn't reveal himself to his brothers right away?
5. Based on Joseph's actions, might we expect that the messianic line would come from him rather than Judah? What's your impression of Judah in this story? What can you learn about God and people based on God's decision to choose Judah over Joseph in the end?
6. Give an example from your own life of Joseph's statement: "You meant evil against me, but God meant it for good" (Gen. 50:20).

Chapter 2 Notes

1 *Testaments of the Twelve Patriarchs*, 1.6.
2 *Genesis Rabbah,* 84:7–13.
3 Francine Prose, "The Story of Joseph in Egypt," in *Genesis As It Is Written: Contemporary Writers on Our First Stories*, ed. David Rosenberg (HarperCollins, 1996), 195.
4 *Jubilees* 34:18–19; cf. Jer. 17:9–10.
5 Herodotus, *Histories*, ii.5.
6 From the inscription of Ankhtifi, ruler of a portion of Upper (southern) Egypt, Stephan Seidlmayer, "The First Intermediate Period," in *The Oxford History of Ancient Egypt,* ed. Ian Shaw (Oxford University Press, 2000), 129.
7 Josephus, *Antiquities of the Jews*, ii.124.
8 1 Maccabees 2:53.
9 *Apostolic Constitutions*, 8.12.24.
10 Ambrose of Milan, *De Joseph Patriarchia.*

Chapter 2 Images

Joseph Receives His Brothers by Francis Bacchiacca, c. 1515
The Travels of Joseph and His Brothers, satellite map courtesy of NASA
Cistern (Paul H. Wright)
Children of Jacob Sell Their Brother Joseph by Konstantin Flavitsky, 1855
Ra (Stig Alenas/Shutterstock)
Egyptians and their neighbors, based on the illustration by Ernst Weidenbach in *Monuments from Egypt and Ethiopia* (1849–1856)
Hyksos juglet, Jerusalem University College (Paul H. Wright)
Hapy, Luxor Temple (CK-Travel Photos/Shutterstock)
Canal along the Nile (Paul H. Wright)
Harvest, Tomb of Menna, The Metropolitan Museum of Art
Pistachios and almonds (Valentina Proskurina/Shutterstock)
The Finding of Joseph's Cup in Benjamin's Sack by Nicolas de Poilly, 1698
Beni-hasan tomb painting (Wikimedia)
Hebron (Paul H. Wright)

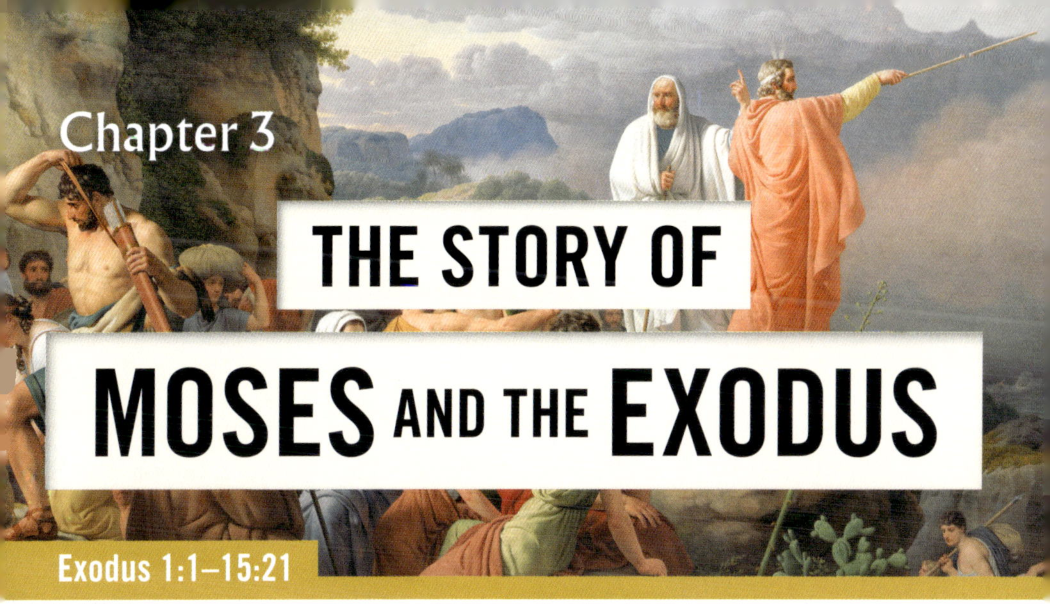

Chapter 3

THE STORY OF MOSES AND THE EXODUS

Exodus 1:1–15:21

THE STORY OF Moses and the exodus from Egypt is an origin story. It is a story that explains how and why God chose Israel to be a special people, then set them on their way to live in fellowship with him in a place they could call their own. It is part of a larger set of origin stories in the Bible that include accounts of the patriarchs, God's revelation on Mount Sinai, Israel's wilderness wanderings, and the entrance into Canaan. Of these, the exodus from Egypt is the key. Without it, we might imagine that God's promises to bless the line of Abraham would lie unfulfilled, that the people of Israel would have been absorbed into the history of a foreign land, and that the messianic line would have withered long before it could ever become a shoot springing "from the stump of Jesse" (Isa. 11:1).

Or so it might seem.

Perhaps the most powerful message of the story of the exodus is that God is able to overcome human foibles and obstinacy and redeem a people to call his own. This tells us that even without the exodus, God would have found a way (as he always does) to fulfill his plans. Yet he chose the miracle that is the exodus, perhaps the most powerful demonstration of God's character recorded in the Old Testament. The story of the exodus is so momentous that it has been deeply woven into the collective memory, and celebration, of God's people ever since.

From baby Moses in the basket to the parting of the sea, the exodus story spans decades, with many gaps and particulars painted only with broad strokes in the text of Scripture. Those fuzzy details have tended to dominate discussions about what actually happened. When was the exodus? What did the plagues look like? How many Israelites crossed the Red Sea? And where did they cross, anyway? These and similar questions can be interesting to pursue (rabbit trails abound) but shouldn't get in the way of the message that the author (and Author) of the story intends to relay. In any case, investigations into the untold details of the exodus story are hampered by a lack of corroborating data from archaeology and Egyptian documents. Remains of buildings or of texts written on papyrus from the wet, low-lying eastern Nile delta where the Israelites lived while in Egypt have nearly completely disappeared, taking with them whatever evidence of Israel's presence at the time of Moses they might have contained. At best we can consider if the exodus account in the Bible is consistent with what is otherwise known of Egyptian history and culture during the second half of the second millennium BC (spoiler alert: it is). But as we seek to understand how the exodus lays the foundational moment in God's unfolding plan of salvation for all humankind, our focus must always return to what we are actually told in the Bible.

The time-worn granite mountains of the southern Sinai Peninsula warmed by the sunrise, as seen from the traditional site of Mount Sinai.

Moses and the Exodus

Themes in the Story of Moses and the Exodus

History has meaning and purpose.

What happens on earth is not a haphazard set of incidents or mere effects caused by the laws of nature. Rather, God is the great "I AM" (Ex. 3:14), a being who is aware of and involved in the affairs of the world, even though at times his will and work are not readily visible to the watching eye. Unlike pagan gods, the Lord God is not a material part of the natural world nor is he limited territorially. Rather, as the single creator he exists outside of and above creation, yet he can enter into it any way and at any time that he pleases. This means that God cares enough to want the best for what he has created and is powerful enough to act both within and beyond the limitations of this world to get it. Human events, the stuff of history, form the arena of divine activity.

God works through the actions of people, even those who are unsure of his presence or unwilling to acknowledge that he exists.

This theme is seen everywhere in the exodus story, from who it is who spies the basket in which the infant Moses lies (Ex. 2:5), to how Aaron actually finds Moses in the vastness of a wilderness where apparently he has never been before (Ex. 4:27), to Pharaoh's incessant stubbornness to not "let my people go" (Ex. 8:1; cf. Ex. 9:16). These and a host of other events might otherwise be seen as fortuitous, predictable, lucky, or happenstance, given the normal circumstances and obligations of life. But throughout the exodus story there is never a time when events are seen to be wholly ordinary and seldom a time when they are construed as wholly supernatural, but most often they are a combination of the two. God sometimes acts through what he has created in ways that help us, when we are too limited to look beyond what is in front of our eyes, to see more fully who he is. In the process, the story of Moses is told in ways that are refreshingly subtle. As an example, consider the wonderfully relevant observation by the first century AD Jewish historian Josephus, commenting on Pharaoh's daughter finding Moses among the rushes of the Nile: "For such was the tender care which God showed for Moses, that the very persons who, by reason of his birth, had decreed the destruction of all children of Hebrew parentage, were made to condescend and nourish and tend him."[1]

God works through nature.

Because God created the world, he can work through it any way that he sees fit. Even though the plagues happen because of the will of God, each involves elements of nature that are well known to the ancient Egyptians. The Red Sea splits, but only after Moses raises his hands and God causes a strong wind to blow all night.

God acts in his own time.

Thanks to cinematography and pop culture, we know the outcome of the exodus even if we've never read the Bible story from beginning to end. But those who were living the events weren't at all sure how it would turn out. Indeed, the exodus story is a textbook example of things getting worse before they get better. God knows that Moses, Israel's deliverer, needed to hone his survival skills in the royal court and the open wilderness before he faced down Pharaoh, though all that the Israelites experience in the meantime is eighty more years of ongoing oppression. God knows that Pharaoh will say "No!" even before he sends Moses to ask. And God knows that even when Pharaoh says "Okay, then go!" he will send in hot pursuit the greatest military force the world had yet known. Nearly always, God allows the situation to slide all the way to "impossible" before he takes visible action—although unbeknownst to the actors, he never fails to prepare the way behind the scenes. Perhaps groaning for deliverance is a necessary part of the process. We can borrow the words of Mordecai spoken to Esther during another impossible time: "And who knows whether you [Moses!] have not come to the kingdom for such a time as this?" (Est. 4:14).

God wants to redeem people from oppression.

Oppression is sometimes physical, sometimes institutional, sometimes social, sometimes economic, sometimes mental, sometimes spiritual, and often a combination of these. God has a plan for human lives which unpacks what it means to be blessed by him. This is summarized in Exodus 6:6–8, words spoken by God to Moses on the eve of Moses's first encounter with Pharaoh:

> *I will bring you out from under the burdens of the Egyptians, and I will deliver you from slavery to them, and I will redeem you with an outstretched arm and with great acts of judgment. I will take you to be my people, and I will be your God, and you shall know that I am the* Lord *your God, who has brought you out from under the burdens of the*

> *Egyptians. I will bring you into the land that I swore to give to Abraham, to Isaac, and to Jacob. I will give it to you for a possession. I am the* LORD.

Here we see the fullness of redemption illustrated by a special people who are destined to live in a special land where they will grow as a covenanted community characterized by intimacy and care. In Moses, God remembers his promises to Abraham (Ex. 2:24; cf. Gen. 12:1–3). His work through Jesus to bring redemption and freedom to people oppressed from within surpasses even that (Luke 4:18–19; John 8:32–36; Gal. 5:1; Heb. 3:1–6).

God chooses reluctant prophets, yet he prepares them ahead of time for the tasks of their calling.

When called by God, Amos was a farmer minding his own business (Amos 7:14–15); Isaiah said he was "a man of unclean lips" (Isa. 6:1–7); Jeremiah objected, "I am only a youth" (Jer. 1:4–10); and Jonah didn't say anything—he just got up and ran (Jonah 1:1–3). Moses is the greatest prophet in ancient Israel (Deut. 34:10–12), yet his reluctance for the job is palpable:

- "Who am I that I should go to Pharaoh?" (Ex. 3:11).
- "They will not believe me or listen to my voice" (Ex. 4:1).
- "I am not eloquent.... I am slow of speech and of tongue" (Ex. 4:10).
- "Please send someone else" (Ex. 4:13).
- "Why have you done evil to this people? Why did you ever send me?" (Ex. 5:22).
- "I am of uncircumcised lips. How will Pharaoh listen to me?" (Ex. 6:30).

It is easy to label Moses a temperamental whiner, someone full of self-doubt. But perhaps he simply has a healthy understanding of the limitations of his own talents and gifts. In either case, how might the story have unfolded if Moses's first response to God was a quick, "Of course I can do this. It's about time you asked!"? How ironic! Being raised in the royal court, Moses must have been schooled in Egyptian language, culture, literature, and religion, yet was hesitant to challenge Pharaoh. (Its a whole lot more comfortable just to be silent.) Yet God, knowing that Moses was fluent in the larger cultural world in which he lived, chose him perhaps because he was the one most prepared to speak into it.

Events in the Story of Moses and the Exodus

A Ruthless Oppression EXODUS 1:1–22

The Hebrews are oppressed in Egypt, even to the point of Pharaoh ordering the death of newborn Hebrew boys.

The exodus story begins with a declaration: "Now there arose a new king over Egypt, who did not know Joseph" (Ex. 1:8). This probably signals a change in the ruling dynasty. Many scholars suggest that Joseph was able to rise to power in Egypt because the pharaohs who were ruling the eastern Nile delta, where the Israelites had settled, belonged to the Semitic Hyksos dynasty (c. 1650–1550 BC). The king who does not know Joseph then must have been either a pharaoh of the subsequent Eighteenth Dynasty who ruled from Thebes in Upper (southern) Egypt (c. 1550–1295 BC) or one from the Nineteenth Dynasty (c. 1295–1186 BC) who, like the Hyksos, ruled from the eastern delta. Whoever this new pharaoh was, he feared the

Rameses II, the longest lived pharaoh and perhaps the pharaoh of the exodus

growing population of Israelites in his land, so he worked them "ruthlessly … and made their lives bitter" (Ex. 1:13–14).

Exodus 1:11 notes that their forced labor was put toward building the store cities of Pithom and Raamses. This detail helps us locate where the exodus story took place and also provides important clues as to when. The most likely location of Pithom is Tell Mashkuta, nestled in the depression of Wadi Tumilat in the eastern Nile delta. The city of Raamses is identified as the sprawling site of Tell Qantir, 20 miles (32 km) northwest. Between lay the fertile fields of the land of Goshen, the geographical center of the Hebrews' settlement in Egypt. Archaeology shows that the city of Raamses was first built as a fort by Seti I (1294–1279 BC), second pharaoh of the Nineteenth Dynasty, then converted to the administrative capital of Egypt by his son, Rameses II (1279–1213 BC). Rameses II was a medgalomaniac, erecting fantastic structures up and down the Nile, with this city, his namesake, the largest of all. Even though very little of the city of Raamses remains today, we can imagine its grandeur by comparing it to other building projects, including his massive mudbrick storeroom complex at the Ramesseum in Upper Egypt, much of which still stands.

Evidence provided by the city of Raamses suggests that the exodus story took place in the thirteenth century BC, a time when the pharaoh would have lived in the same region as the Israelite settlement in Goshen.

Partially reconstructed portion of the grain storerooms at the Ramesseum

Another suggestion is that the exodus was in the fifteenth century BC, even though the pharaohs of that time, the Eighteenth Dynasty, ruled from Thebes, 300 miles (500 km) south. Scholars who hold to this earlier date base their calculations on 1 Kings 6:1, which states that Solomon began to build the Jerusalem temple in the fourth year of his reign, 480 years after the exodus. In examining both positions, we must ask this question: Did the ancients calculate time in the same way that we do today, or might the figure 480 (as 40 x 12) simply be a way of indicating that 12 generations of indeterminate length had passed between the events? (The number 40 is sometimes used in texts from the ancient Near East to indicate a generation.)

Israel's experience under the new king of Egypt "who did not know Joseph" was one of slavery. Given the forms of slavery that plague the world today or those that have infected our shared recent past, it is fair to ask the question, "What was slavery like in the time of Moses?" Chattel slavery as known in the West (including the appalling history of the United States), where masses of people are brought from foreign lands to live without personal rights and to breed other slaves, was largely unknown in the ancient Near East. In Egypt, prisoners of war, people picked up by merchants on their foreign travels, or resident aliens who had

THE HEBREWS

The Israelites are often called "Hebrews" in the story of the exodus (Ex. 1:15; 2:13; 5:3). The word *Hebrew* seems to be an outsider term, since it almost always occurs in the Bible when the Israelites are living in a foreign context or when foreigners speak of the Israelites, even when they are at home. Scholars debate the etymology of the term; it is likely derived from the verb *'eber*, "to go beyond," and may mean "the one from beyond," that is, from the outside. When speaking to each other, the Israelites call themselves "sons of Israel," a kinship-based insider term.

fallen into debt were reduced to various levels of servitude. The personal rights which they were able to maintain varied with the time, place, and circumstance of their servitude. We recall that the Hebrew word *'ebed* can be translated as either "slave" or "servant," depending on the context and that sometimes the line dividing the two is rather blurry. Typical jobs for those in servitude were to cultivate land, work in construction, serve in the army, or serve domestically. Paintings in the tomb of Rekhmire, vizier of Pharaoh Thutmose III (1479–1425 BC), depict foreign slaves making bricks, but plenty of written evidence from the time of Rameses II (1279–1213 BC) attests to this kind of slavery as well.

Work quotas were common in ancient Egypt for both Egyptians and non-Egyptians alike, as were hard taskmasters and rebellious slaves. This is certainly the case for Israel at the time of Moses (Ex. 5:10–21). But a close reading of the exodus story reveals that the Israelites in Egypt have something to fall back on. On the material side, it seems that they maintain rights of ownership and use. For instance, the Bible notes that the plagues do not harm the livestock owned by the Israelites (Ex. 9:6); and when they leave Egypt, they take their own flocks, herds, kitchen equipment, and

Brickmakers, depicted in the tomb of Rekhmire (c. 1479–1425 BC), vizier of Pharaoh Thutmose III, a candidate for the pharaoh who oppressed Israel

clothing from their own houses with them (Ex. 12:32, 34, 38; Deut. 29:5). We also read that before leaving Egypt, each household sacrifices one of its own lambs at Passover, a feast they celebrated without asking the Egyptian authorities for permission (Ex. 12:3, 31–34). All of this indicates that the Israelites living in Egypt as slaves own property with the right to use it as they see fit, something that chattel slaves are denied. But more important than these material things, the Israelites have a covenant relationship with a God who hears their groaning and cares to do something utterly dramatic about it. But in the meantime, Israel's life in Egypt, a land not their own, is at the harsh beck and call of Pharaoh, a king not their own, and they long to be free in a land of their own.

THE MIDWIVES

We know from Scripture the names of the midwives, Shiphrah and Puah, who attend the Israelite birthing mothers (Ex. 1:15), but we don't know the name of Pharaoh, the most powerful man in Egypt. The midwives are remembered; Pharaoh remains anonymous. Their brave actions saving babies from Pharaoh's infanticidal decree are the first recorded example of civil disobedience for a righteous cause in ancient literature.

Moses—Hebrew, Egyptian, and Midianite EXODUS 2:1–25

Moses is born, set adrift in a basket to avoid infanticide by Pharaoh, then raised in the royal household. He flees to Midian after killing an Egyptian foreman who is beating an Israelite.

Like the Hebrew midwives, the mother of Moses finds a way to save her child. She carefully places him in a basket among the reeds of the riverbank where he will be found. The pitch-coated papyrus basket in which Moses floats is a *tevah*, an Egyptian loanword used only elsewhere in the Bible for Noah's ark. Both vessels, radically different in size, are guided only by God, who saves their occupants from otherwise certain death.

Pharaoh's very own daughter discovers the Hebrew infant, adopts him, and names him Moses (Ex. 2:10). The meaning of the name Moses seems to be a bilingual word play. In Hebrew, Moses sounds like the verb *mashah*, "to draw out," appropriate for someone who is drawn out of the water and ends up drawing all of Israel out of Egypt through the Red Sea. In Egyptian, the name Moses probably comes from the verb *msi*, "to give birth to," which was frequently an element in longer names declaring that certain gods had given birth to individuals; for example, Thut*mose* suggests someone "the god Thoth bore." Moses was raised in the Egyptian court, and we might expect that the Egyptians would have wanted his name to be attached to the name of an Egyptian deity. That it wasn't is a clue that even when he otherwise was immersed in Egyptian society, growing up with all of the malleable impressions of youth, Moses kept his identity as a God-fearing Israelite.

Ancient Egyptian storage basket made of halfa grass and palm leaf

The land of Midian, the place to which Moses flees after he kills an Egyptian whom he catches beating an Israelite, lay primarily east of the Gulf of Aqaba/Gulf of Eilat, the northeastern arm of the Red Sea. Because the Midianites were a wide-ranging group of people involved in shepherding and long-distance trade (their ancestors had brought Joseph to Egypt), we might expect to find them in other places as well, such as west of the Gulf of Aqaba and even in the interior of the Sinai Peninsula (Gen. 37:28, 36; Isa. 60:6). The Midianites were descended from Abraham and Keturah, making them long-distant Semitic cousins of Moses (Gen. 25:1–2).

Isaac, Jacob, Joseph, and Moses all marry women from distant lands. Rebekkah, Leah, and Rachel are cousins of their spouses, Isaac and

Jacob, something consistent with the custom of the time, which favored marriage within tight family groups. The wives of Joseph and Moses, on the other hand, are daughters of pagan priests, true foreigners (Gen. 41:45; Ex. 2:16, 21; Num. 12:1). Medieval Jewish commentary holds that both Zipporah and Jethro, Moses's wife and father-in-law, gave up their pagan ways even before Moses arrived at their well, making everything kosher.[2] But the Bible is silent on details of Moses's private life. Still, it uses the circumstances of Moses's marriage to provide an example of how God chooses whom he wants, from whatever background he or she may happen to be (we recall Rahab the Canaanite and Ruth the Moabite who are part of the family tree of Jesus; Matt. 1:5).

Having spent forty years in the Egyptian royal court, Moses spends another forty years as a Midian-based shepherd, getting in touch with a desert landscape that teaches him wilderness survival skills (Ex. 7:7; Acts 7:23). He will use what he learns later as he shepherds Israel for forty more years through much of the same barren and howling wasteland (Deut. 32:10; cf. Pss. 78:52–54; 106:9–23).

A Holy Mountain EXODUS 3:1–4:31

Moses encounters the Lord God at a burning bush at Horeb. God commissions Moses to bring the Israelites out of Egypt and lead them to the land of Canaan. Moses returns to Egypt with his family.

The name Horeb, the mountain where Moses meets God at the burning bush, means, appropriately, "desolation" or "wasteland." It seems to be an alternate name for Mount Sinai and perhaps also designates the region of the mountain (Ex. 3:1; 19:1–2, 20; 1 Kings 19:8). Interpreters generally agree that Horeb is the same mountain where Moses will receive the Ten Commandments (Ex. 3:12). Some recent interpreters favor a site for Horeb/Mount Sinai in the Arabian Peninsula, east of the Red Sea, within the heartland of Midian, primarily because Galatians 4:25 refers to "Mount Sinai in Arabia." This suggestion is countered by a host of Greek

Sunrise from Jebel Musa. The Gulf of Eilat and Arabian mountains line the horizon.

and Latin authors from the time of the New Testament who use the name Arabia to include all of what is now the Sinai Peninsula, as far west as the border of Egypt.[3] While the traditional site of Mount Sinai, Jebel Musa in the high granite massif in the southern Sinai Peninsula, was codified as the location of Mount Sinai by Christian monks only in the sixth century AD, we must remember that they looked for clues in the Bible with the same eye for literal detail that is valued by interpreters today.

Nearly all traditional interpreters understand the bush that was alight with fire but not consumed, to have been a thorn bush or bramble bush, hence a harsh plant that adds to the raw enigma of the moment. Dried by the hyperarid climate, the plant should have been fully consumed in an instant. Commentaries are full of naturalistic explanations—it was really a nearby campfire, the reflection of sunlight on red leaves, a plant that secretes flammable oils, or something else that tricked even the wilderness-wise Moses—but the story is meant, in no uncertain terms, to describe an event that is totally unexplainable, a wholly consuming holy moment. Fire is often connected to God's revealed presence in the Bible, something mysterious, dangerous, unapproachable, self-perpetuating, purifying, and radiant (Ex. 24:17; Deut. 4:11–12; 1 Kings 18:38; 2 Chron. 7:1–3; Ps. 18:12–13; Ezek. 1:4, 27–28; Dan. 7:9–10; Heb. 12:29).

Many interpreters suggest that Moses's question to God—"What is [your] name?" (Ex. 3:13)—implies that he is not asking for a nametag but rather the quality, character, and essence of the Deity; not "*Who* are you" but "Who *are* you?" In response, God reveals his personal name: in Hebrew, *'Ehyeh-'Asher-'Ehyeh*. Our first question is "How can this name be translated into English?" Suggestions abound, full of nuance: "I am who I am;" "I am what I am;" "I am because I am;" "I am that I am;" "I am who I will be;" "I will be who I will be;" "I may be who I may be;" "I am the existing one;" "I create what I create;" "It is I who am with you and I who always am." Most scholars suggest that this sentence-name stems from the Hebrew verb *haya*, "to be," melding as one the realities that God exists, is present, cares, and never changes (cf. Deut. 11:12; Rev. 4:8). It is from this verb "to be" that God's personal name derives, written both as YHWH and LORD. The name shows that God is ontologically (of essence) different from the gods of Egypt that saturate the land where Moses and the Israelites live. The intent of God's self-revelation at the burning bush is not to obscure himself as a being who is unapproachable and harsh, but rather it is a positive, life-embracing response to Moses's inquiry. The bush, which after all should have been consumed, continues to live.

Moses encountering God at the burning bush

God renews with Moses the covenant promises that he had made to Abraham, Isaac, and Jacob (Ex. 3:6–8, 16–17; 6:2–8). Israel is not just leaving Egypt but going to "a land flowing with milk and honey" (Ex. 3:8; cf. Deut. 8:7–9; 11:10–12). With these promises in tow, Moses knows that he belongs somewhere other than in Egypt and to someone other than Pharaoh.

The event following this episode is only three verses long, but it's probably the most enigmatic of the entire exodus story: On their way to Egypt, Moses's wife quickly circumcises their son to stop the Lord from killing Moses (Ex. 4:24–26). While it's not possible to know the exact reason from the scant details provided, it does front the place of circumcision as a sign of belonging to God's covenanted people, instituted first with Abraham (Gen. 17:1–14). Once Israel enters Canaan, circumcision will mark Israel as a special people, serving to distinguish them physically from their uncircumcised neighbors, especially the Philistines (1 Sam. 17:26). But the Egyptians also practiced circumcision, prompting us to ask an unanswerable question: Is there a visible, practical outcome of circumcision for the Israelites at *this* point in their history, or is it only a symbol of something internal?

The Ten Plagues EXODUS 5:1–11:10

With God's power, Moses and Aaron call down ten plagues upon Egypt. The plagues are increasingly catastrophic to the Egyptians' livelihood and challenge the power and authority of Pharaoh. But Pharaoh's heart remains hard.

The opening scene in this episode finds Moses and Aaron in the presence of Pharaoh. We are given no explanation as to how Moses gains access to the king, nor why Pharaoh should care to have a conversation with a wanted man who had fled Egypt forty years earlier, his prior connection to Pharaoh's daughter notwithstanding. This is an example of how a close reading of the text reveals a myriad of details left unsaid, prompting us, the readers, to pose questions that beg to be asked but have no clear answer. In the process, we enter into the story. Pharaoh's initial reply is wholly expected: "Who is the Lord, that I should obey his voice?" (Ex. 5:2). Prompted to ask the same question ourselves, Pharaoh's retort anticipates the way that the rest of the exodus story reveals who "the Lord" actually is (Ex. 8:19; 9:20, 27; 10:7).

Pharaoh's question, "Who is the Lord?" is initially answered in Exodus 6:6–8, a fourfold revelation of God's personal promise to Israel:

I will bring you out of Egypt, deliver you from bondage, redeem you with an outstretched arm, and take you for my people.

The Egyptian magicians who seek to replicate the acts of Moses are as nameless as Pharaoh (Ex. 7:11; 8:7). Yet early interpreters wanted details, so in the first century BC the Damascus Document, a Hebrew text found in Egypt, called them Jannes and Jambres, mentioning that they were in league with the Belial, the devil.[4] This tradition is relayed in 2 Timothy 3:8.

The phrase that Pharaoh's heart became hard occurs nineteen times in the exodus story. Nine times, we read, Pharaoh either hardens his own heart or his heart "was hardened," apparently of his own volition (Ex. 7:13–14, 22; 8:15, 19, 32; 9:7, 34–35). Then, ten times God hardens Pharaoh's heart (Ex. 4:21; 7:3; 9:12; 10:1, 20, 27; 11:10; 14:4, 8, 17). The timing is important: Pharaoh hardens his own heart in spite of the first five plagues, while God hardens Pharaoh's heart starting with the plague of boils, the first plague that touches Pharaoh's person. God follows up the sixth plague by saying that the only reason Pharaoh is still on the throne is so that Pharaoh can witness God's power, yet God continues to give Pharaoh chances to repent (Ex. 9:16–17).

The question of predestination versus free will, which occupies our theologies today, isn't resolved in this story. Yet a careful reading shows that God starts to harden Pharaoh's heart only after Pharaoh's own culpability in refusing to change is clearly demonstrated. The process is a confirmation of the natural outworking of human sin.

The ten plagues fall in a generally ascending order of severity on Egypt:

- Pharaoh's magicians are able to duplicate the effect of the first two plagues but not the third.
- Starting with the third, the plagues fall on the Egyptians only, while the Israelites are spared.
- The plagues affect first the Nile which flows through Egypt; then the land, crops, and cattle from which the Egyptians earn their livelihood; then their homes.

Because the plagues involve elements of the environment of Egypt, scholars have long attempted to understand them as normal—though excessive—processes of nature, with each effect becoming the cause of the next plague. Some have suggested that the plagues sprang from seasonal environmental changes over the course of the year—from the Nile turning red as it rose in July, carrying microorganisms in its wake, to the sky darkening from blowing dust the next spring. If we think naturalistically, there is some merit in these suggestions, and God sometimes does choose to use elements of nature to awaken his inattentive people. Yet the sole explanation for each plague given in the biblical account is the will of God, accompanied, sometimes, by the outstretched hand of Moses.

It is important to note that the plagues do not involve mythical creatures acting in superhuman ways. In this way the Bible is credible when compared to other ancient Near Eastern religious texts which speak in mythic, superhero terms when describing their founding events.[5] At the same time, because the plagues involve elements of nature, they speak directly to the Egyptian mythological structure of the universe in which gods are conceived to be part and parcel of specific naturalistic forces.[6] Over these gods, as their representative on earth, stands Pharaoh, whose primary responsibility is to ensure *ma'at,* cosmic balance and harmony. By opposing the Lord, Pharaoh seeks to ensure his own control over not just Egypt but the entire universe. In defeating the power that Pharaoh claims to have over nature, God not only proves his control over human will but shows that true authority lies in a single Deity. Commenting on the clause "on all the gods of Egypt I will execute judgments" (Ex. 12:12), Jewish interpreters in the mid-first millennium AD concluded that the plagues were aimed foremost at the gods of Egypt, saying "God will not punish a people until he first punishes [or discredits] their gods."[7]

The Egyptian belief that elements of their natural environment were personified, or represented, in specific gods is visible in several of the ten plagues. All of the plagues attack the economic self-sufficiency of Egypt.

1. Nile Blood (Ex. 7:14–25)

While some interpreters hold that the Nile turned to real blood, most suggest that "blood" should be read idiomatically as the color red (as it is in Joel 2:31). Before the Nile was dammed in modern times, its annual flooding began in July. In years of exceptionally high flooding, the floodwaters carried large amounts of red soils and reddish flagellates picked up in Ethiopia and the Sudanese swamps, cutting the oxygen level of the water and making it unhealthy for fish and human consumption alike. In such years, the Egyptians held that the god of the Nile inundation, Hapy, who was a capricious deity, acted malevolently. In any case, the first the plague completely discredits Hapy, the purported bringer of renewed life.

2. Frogs (Ex. 8:1–15)

Each year, as frogs jumped from the receding Nile into the silt-enriched fields along its banks, Egyptians honored *Heqet*, the frog goddess, for rebirthing the land. In this plague, the entire country is overrun by the green hoppers, and when they, representing the goddess of life, all die, infection and disease spread into the houses of the Egyptians. Said Josephus, the country was "saturated with their horrible slime."[8]

3. Gnats/Mosquitoes (Ex. 8:16–19)

Scholars debate the identity of these tiny pests: Are they gnats, carried by the blowing sand? Or mosquitoes, breeding in the stagnant pools left as the waters recede? Both were common to ancient Egypt—and equally irritating.

4. Flies (Ex. 8:20–32)

These are swarms of flies, probably the biting kind, likely disease-borne after feeding on the decaying bodies of frogs.

5. Plague on Livestock (Ex. 9:1–7)

Whatever its precise identification (some suggest anthrax originating in the red-soiled Nile and exacerbated by decaying frogs and biting flies), this pestilence signals that the plagues are no longer just irritating, but they attack the livelihood and food supply of the Egyptians.

6. Boils (Ex. 9:8–12)

This plague may be infected blisters, smallpox, anthrax, or ulcers. With it, the plagues become personal. (The final plague to hit Job, during which he scrapes himself with a piece of pottery to reduce the pain as he sits in ashes, seems to be something similar; Job 2:4–8.)

7. Hailstones (Ex. 9:13–35)

Hailstones decimate the fields of ripe flax and barley, sparing the wheat and spelt, which are not yet mature. This places the plague in late winter or early spring.

8. Locusts (Ex. 10:1–20)

Swarms of locusts have long been the scourge of the Middle East, sweeping into arable lands from the deserts of Sudan and the Arabian Peninsula. Locusts come in several varieties, all with voracious appetites, and together they can strip every green blade from a springtime field (cf. Joel 1:4, 10). In this plague, the locusts ensure that whatever crops the hailstones failed to hit are stripped of all nutritional value. The economic power of Egypt, rooted in the annual grain harvest, is wrecked, with famine, hunger, and starvation up and down the Nile sure to follow.

9. Darkness (Ex. 10:21–29)

Because the darkness of the ninth plague lasted for three days, it could not have been an eclipse, as some interpreters suggest. Most scholars understand the darkness as being caused by a *hamsin*, a hot, dry wind common in early spring that whips up dust and fine sand. At its worst, a *hamsin* blocks out the sunlight and turns the sky to a dark sandy-brown. The effect on people and animals alike is palatable, sucking moisture from gritty bodies and grating the mind. People stay indoors since it is a darkness that literally can be felt (Ex. 10:21).

With the plague of darkness, the vigorous, all-pervading head of the Egyptian pantheon, the sun god Amun-Ra, has disappeared. This is a terrifying foreshadowing of what is next, for spirits of death in ancient Egypt were thought to be more active at night.

10. Death of the Firstborn (Ex. 11:4–10; 12:29–32)

This plague destroys not only Pharaoh's planned royal succession but the progeny, continuity, future, and hope of every Egyptian family.

The First Passover EXODUS 12:1–13:16

Israel's last supper in Egypt is the Passover, eaten in homes marked with the blood of each Passover lamb so that the angel of death, who is executing the plague, will pass over, or spare, their firstborn.

As they are about to exit Egypt and become a new people, the Israelites are given a new calendar, one that reckons the beginning of the year in the spring month of Abib (Nisan) rather than starting the year in the summer as their Egyptian neighbors do or in the autumn like the Canaanites (Ex. 12:2; 23:15). The Israelite holidays, which celebrate the greatest events in their founding history, are all fixed to times in that calendar that corresponded to the agricultural cycle of Canaan, the land to which Moses and the people are heading:

- Passover (*Pesach*) at the beginning of the barley harvest in early spring, celebrating the exodus from Egypt;
- Weeks (*Shavuot* or Pentecost) at the wheat harvest in late spring, celebrating the law (Torah) given on Mount Sinai; and
- Tabernacles or Booths (*Succot*) at the autumn harvest of summer fruit, celebrating God's care during the wilderness wanderings.

The Israelites of the first Passover are instructed to "eat the flesh [of the lambs] that night, roasted on the fire; with unleavened bread and bitter herbs" and to "eat it in haste" (Ex. 12:8–11, 34). Scholars suggest that there is something more to the instruction that Israel bake their Passover bread without leaven than just the need to flee Goshen more quickly than the time it takes for bread to rise, since that reason is only implied and not specifically given in the story. The New Testament ties the act of leavening, or being leavened, to corruption, perhaps because leavening involves fermentation, an active breakdown (and then transformation) of the dough (Matt. 16:6; 1 Cor. 5:6–8; Gal. 5:9).[9] Scholars think that leaven was invented in Egypt; perhaps eating unleavened bread, like changing the calendar and demonstrating that the Egyptian deities are ineffective, is a way for Israel to say, "We don't belong here anymore."

Unleavened bread

A Way Made by God EXODUS 13:17–15:21

Israel leaves Egypt, but their route takes them to a point where they are trapped between Pharaoh's army and the Red Sea. God parts the waters of the sea so that Israel can cross; then the waters return to drown the Egyptian army.

The Egyptians are anxious for Israel leave quickly, yet they also treat Israel with favor in allowing them to take whatever they want as they go, including clothing, gold, and silver (Ex. 12:33, 36). This was the Lord's doing, but probably also reflects genuine attitudes among at least some of the people, since the Egyptians and Israelites had been living with each other for centuries. In any case, the Israelites leave with resolve, no longer weakened by bondage (Ex. 3:21–22; 11:2–3; 12:33–36). Once in the wilderness, the Israelites will help build the tabernacle and its implements by contributing from these goods (Ex. 25:1–9). Abraham, too, had left

Egypt, having gained great wealth while there (Gen. 12:16; 13:2).

Scholars energetically debate the number of people who leave Egypt with Moses. Commentaries often report two to three million people, an estimate calculated from Exodus 12:37, which reports that the number totals "six hundred thousand men on foot, besides women and children." This is a very large number to have been served by just two midwives (Ex. 1:15), and it assumes an astronomical birthrate coupled with an unreasonably low rate of infant mortality during Israel's years in Egypt, since Jacob's family had numbered only seventy persons when they entered (Ex. 1:5). Looking outside the story itself, three million people is equal to nearly half the entire population of ancient Egypt, far more than the small land of Goshen could support or the people of Egypt control. Moreover, the logistical issues of moving a mass of people that large through the Sinai are immense (the population of the Sinai today, minus the tourist towns along the coast, is only a few tens of thousands of people). The subsequent story of the wilderness wanderings recognizes that the hyperarid Sinai can't produce enough water and food for everyone and that there are too many people for Moses to judge their personal affairs all alone (Ex. 15:22–18:27), but two to three million people defies even this explanation.

One popular suggestion to try to understand how many people left Egypt is to consider the meaning of the Hebrew word *eleph*, "thousand," in Exodus 12:37. The same word can also mean a "military unit" or "family clan" of a much smaller size (e.g., Judg. 6:15; 1 Sam. 10:19; 17:18). In this case, the phrase 600 *eleph* may not mean 600,000 people but rather 600 family units, from which we can estimate perhaps 20,000 people. While specifics are elusive (we just don't know how the ancients recorded this kind of data), the intent of the text is clear: It's a lot of people, and they are not going to be able to survive the journey through the wilderness to Canaan on their own.

But once the Israelites are on their way to freedom, Pharaoh changes his mind—and heart—again: "'What is this we have done, that we have let Israel go from serving us?' So he made ready his chariot and took his army with him" (Ex. 14:5–6). Pharaoh's chariot corps had the reputation as the strongest and most effective in the ancient Near East. It was typically led by the crown prince, but in this case, since the crown prince perishes in the tenth plague, it may be led by Pharaoh himself. We know from Egyptian records that none of the pharaohs of Egypt drowned in the Red Sea. This is consistent with the biblical account, which states only that Pharaoh's chariots and army are destroyed (Ex. 14:28; 15:4).

Rameses II in full battle array, depicted in the Ramesseum

Scholars debate the location where Moses and all Israel cross the sea to escape Pharaoh's army. Several things complicate the discussion. One is that the Hebrew term for the sea that they cross is *yam suf*, "sea of reeds," a name that fits one of the shallow, reedy saltwater lakes directly east of Goshen on the northwestern corner of the Sinai Peninsula. But the Bible also calls the much deeper, reedless body of water on the opposite side of the Sinai Peninsula, what is today called the Gulf of Aqaba/Gulf of Eilat, an arm of the Red Sea, *yam suf* (e.g., Ex. 23:31; 1 Kings 9:26). We do not know why the Bible calls both bodies of water, which are very different not only in their location but also in their geographical character, by the same name. The English translation "Red Sea" is not a Hebrew term but comes from the Septuagint, the Greek translation of the Hebrew Old Testament in the third century BC. We also don't know why the Septuagint translated *yam suf* as Red Sea; perhaps it was because the Gulf of Aqaba reflects the reddish color of the granite and sandstone mountains that line its shore. In any case, a plain reading of the exodus account places the location of the crossing of the sea somewhere in close proximity to Goshen, on a route that chariots can follow, not at a body of water located across 200 miles (320 km) of a rugged, hyperarid landscape. A shallow sea of reeds fits the Bible's description that the waters parted due to a strong east wind combined, of course, with the raised staff of Moses (Ex. 14:16, 21).

The question "Where was the Red Sea?" is often tied to the location of Mount Sinai, and here there is no compelling reason to seek that location outside of the Sinai Peninsula. Purported discoveries of submerged chariot wheels or a land bridge across the Gulf of Aqaba are things of discredited photos and geological imagination. But we might ask, if the Red Sea were a smallish lake, why don't the Israelites just go around it? Here the only explanation is that God again wants to show his power and confirm Moses as a leader that Israel can trust in impossible situations. We can also picture the chariots in such close pursuit that Moses doesn't have time to circle around. Josephus explained the situation clearly: "The Hebrews were left with no prospect but that of utter destruction," and then he followed up by saying they passed through "a God-sent road."[10]

The last time that Moses was in the Sinai Peninsula he was tentative and hesitant. As he heads back in, he is fully confident not only in his ability to lead the people of Israel through "that great and terrifying wilderness" that lies ahead (Deut. 1:19) but confident also of the mighty hand of God that will lead him all the way.

The story of the exodus from Egypt ends here, but the story of Moses and the sons of Israel continues through the rest of the Pentateuch. The exodus event anticipates the forthcoming challenges and provision that Israel will experience on their journey to Mount Sinai and their forty-year trek through the wilderness to Canaan.

"Moses stretched out his hand over the sea, and the LORD drove the sea back by a strong east wind" (Ex. 14:21).

MOSES IN LATER WRITINGS

The exodus becomes a prominent theme in the rest of the Old Testament, reminding Israel of their identity and the character of God:

- It is remembered at key moments in Israel's history as the basis for God's ongoing acts of redemption (Josh. 2:10; 24:2–7; 1 Sam. 10:18–19; 1 Kings 8:53; 2 Kings 17:7; Neh. 9:9–12).
- Because the Psalms sing about the exodus, we know that celebrating it was an active part of temple liturgy (Pss. 78; 80; 81; 105; 106; 136).
- The prophets speak about the exodus to encourage Israel to live in ways that are consistent with what it means to be redeemed (Isa. 43:16–20; 48:21–22; Jer. 2:6; Ezek. 20:5–10; Mic. 6:3–4).

The writers of the New Testament are eager to show that Jesus is like Moses—but greater:

- Jesus sojourns in Egypt, then leaves for his home in the land of Israel (Matt. 2:14–15; cf. Hos. 11:1). Coptic (Egyptian Christian) theology is rich in traditions that the holy family fled for their lives from the Romans up and down the Nile, reminiscent of the treatment Israel faced from Pharaoh.
- Moses appears on a new mount of revelation, the mount of Transfiguration, hearing the voice of God proclaim that because Jesus is the Son of God, everyone (even Moses) should listen to *him* (Matt. 17:1–5).
- The Passover celebration was the most significant annual festival for Jews in the time of the New Testament, a powerful glue binding them into a single people worldwide. That Jesus was crucified in Jerusalem at Passover is a clear statement that it is he who brings redemption. Jesus is both the unblemished sacrificial lamb and the firstborn Son who is slain just after darkness envelops the land (Matt. 27:45; John 1:29; 1 Cor. 5:7; 1 Peter 1:17–21; Rev. 5:12). The Passover celebration, redefined by the death and resurrection of Jesus, was the only annual Christian celebration during the first 150 years of the church.

- Moses is a faithful servant worthy of great honor, surpassed only by Christ (Heb. 3:1–6). The writer of Hebrews explains that the things that happened to Moses happened "by faith" and in expectation of Christ, the Messiah, in whom the promises would be complete (Heb. 11:23–29, 39–40).
- The apostle Paul likens the passage through the Red Sea to baptism (1 Cor. 10:1–2).

Because of the general feelings of anti-Semitism that permeated the Roman world in the time of the New Testament, Greek and Latin writers of the first century AD who mentioned Moses as a lawgiver to the Jews tended to portray him in an unfavorable light. For example, Quintilian and Tacitus said that Moses's laws were harmful, promoting "practices that were opposed to all other men."[11] Other pagan sources portrayed Moses as a magician or someone who opposed "true religion" (i.e., Greek and Roman religion).

To counter these and similar ideas, Philo, a Jewish scholar living in Alexandria, Egypt, wrote in his *Life of Moses* that Moses was actually the inspiration for all Greek philosophy, an ideal priest, prophet, king, and leader of people. Josephus, the Jewish historian who wrote *Antiquities of the Jews* while living in Rome at the end of the first century AD, similarly had nothing but praise for Moses's physical appearance, talents, abilities, chivalry, and accomplishments, elaborating his life with superlatives at every turn.

The story of the exodus from Egypt has been fertile literary ground ever since, interpreted and reinterpreted in sermons and writings through the centuries. For the church fathers, Israel's journey through the wilderness became a model of the Christian life, a life freed from sin and rewarded by life in the heavenly promised land. For many Europeans entangled in oppressive economic and political systems in the Age of Enlightenment, the Protestant Reformation spurred immigration to the New World, envisioned as a promised land in which they, like Moses, could create a new, free society. For enslaved Africans in America, the hope of freedom in a new promised land was the focus of activism, sermon, and song—and remains so for their descendants even today.

Study Questions

1. How is the story of the exodus an origin story? What does it begin?
2. How does the story of Moses show us that God can work through the actions of people who are either unsure of his presence or unwilling to acknowledge that he exists? Give an example from your own experience.
3. To what extent can (or should) we use the exodus story as confirmation that God wants to deliver all people from all manner of oppression today?
4. What does the story of the exodus teach us about who God is? Consider especially what God reveals about himself to Moses at the burning bush.
5. If you were a Hebrew slave in Egypt, what might you have thought about the plagues as they occurred—and what might you have thought if you were an ancient Egyptian?
6. How is the exodus from Egypt remembered in the rest of the Old Testament? In the New Testament? And today?

Chapter 3 Notes

1 Josephus, *Antiquities of the Jews*, ii.225.
2 Rashi's commentary on Exodus 2:16.
3 For example, Herodotus *Histories,* ii, 12; Strabo *Geography,* xvii, 1, 21; Polyaenus *Stratagems,* vii, ii, 7; Aristides *Orations,* 36, 87; Basilius *Caesariensis Homiliae* in *Hexaemeron,* iv, PG 29, col 88.
4 The Damascus Document was discovered in the Cairo Geniza, a repository for scrolls in the Ben Ezra synagogue in Old Cairo, Egypt, in 1897. Fragments of the Damascus Document were also found in the caves of Qumran, linking it to the Dead Sea Scrolls.
5 In the Babylonian creation myth, Enuma Elish, the storm god Marduk kills the primordial goddess of the sea, Tiamat, then creates the elemental parts of the world out of her dismembered body. In one Egyptian creation story, the god of fertility, Osiris, is killed by Seth, the god of the desert, then avenged by his son, Horus, the god of kingship. Both Marduk in Babylon and Horus in Egypt became the deities who justified the right of kings to rule over their human realms.
6 Ancient Near Eastern creation stories typically depict deities as personifications of the very elements of nature that they, or their deity parents, create. For instance, the Egyptian god of the sun, Ra, rose from a primordial chaos and gave birth by himself to the god of the air and the goddess of moisture. They in turn bore the god of the earth and the goddess of the sky.
7 Tanhuma B, 14; Exodus Rabah 9:10.
8 Josephus, *Antiquities of the Jews*, ii.297.
9 See also the Babylonian Talmud, *Berakhoth* 17a.
10 Josephus, Antiquities of the Jews, ii.326, 339.
11 Quintilian, *Institutes of Oratory*, 3.7.21; Tacitus, *Histories*, 5.4–5.

Chapter 3 Images

Israelites Crossing the Red Sea by Christoffer Eckersberg, 1815
Sinai mountains (Paul H. Wright)
Moses and the Exodus; satellite map courtesy of NASA
Visage of Rameses II, temple of Luxor (Paul H. Wright)
Storeroom at Ramesseum (Iurii Kazakov/Shutterstock)
Brickmakers, Tomb of Rekhmire, The Metropolitan Museum of Art
Egyptian basket, The Metropolitan Museum of Art
Jebel Musa sunrise (Paul H. Wright)
Moses icon, St. Catherine's Monastery (Olha Solodenko/Shutterstock)
Unleavened bread (Africa Studio/Shutterstock)
Rameses II in battle, the Ramesseum, Luxor (Paul H. Wright)
Moses (godongphoto/Shutterstock)

Chapter 4

THE STORY OF RUTH

Ruth 1–4

THE STORY OF Ruth is uplifting, something to feel good about. But in describing it this way, it would be a mistake to label it a "feel good story," for that trivializes the very real difficulties already present in the opening line, not to mention those that plague its heroes as the drama unfolds. The story carries us from tragedy to hope to resolution as Naomi and her daughter-in-law Ruth seek—and then find—security in life at home.

The focus of the story is on people who act how we hope all of us will when facing immense difficulty. That is summarized by the Hebrew term *ḥesed*, which appears at two key moments in the story. The first is on the lips of Naomi who describes the redemptive actions of Boaz (Ruth 2:20). The second is by Boaz, expressing awe at the faithful conduct of Ruth (Ruth 3:10). Often translated as "kindness," "lovingkindness," or "mercy," *ḥesed* embodies an unbreakable bond of loyalty, person to person, or people to God. What this can mean in real life is illustrated in Ruth's story by examples of life lived *ḥesed-ly.*

But there is more. As we read, we see that the story of Ruth is an intimate and, we must assume, accurate view of cultural norms that shaped the early settlement days of ancient Israel prior to the rise of kingship under David. It is, in fact, one of the most important windows revealing family rights and responsibilities in biblical Israel. The smallest unit in ancient Israelite society was not the individual, as it is in the modern

West, but the nuclear family, an entity called the "father's house," *bet av* (Gen. 24:23, 38; Judg. 14:15; 19:2; Isa. 22:23; John 14:2). This term and its cultural associations are common in patriarchal societies. The land of Israel was set in an arena not particularly well resourced for a comfortable life. To counter its harsh living conditions, the Israelites, living in a patriarchal society, developed survival mechanisms focused on tight family relationships under the authority of the oldest close male relative. The primary responsibility of this patriarch was to ensure provision and protection for everyone under his care. Women living in patriarchal societies tended to be resilient and resourceful, with avenues to act for the common good in creative, powerful ways. In reading the story of Ruth, we shouldn't think that what it has to tell us must be provincial and outdated because of the overriding views of patriarchy today, most of which focus on individuality and sexism. Provision and protection are big-world interests after all, no matter when or where we live. The biblical term for a full, safe, and secure life is *shalom*, something that Jesus defines as "life [lived] abundantly" and which, in the end, only he can bring (John 10:10). But in the meantime, the story of Ruth depicts what all of this means given the on-the-ground norms and expectations of life in early Israel (Ruth 3:1).

The story of Ruth is a story of common people. Absent are the glorious deeds of generals, kings, or priests. Nor are there miracles in the story, visions or visits by God, or moments of grand revelation. What we see instead are the normal activities of real people doing expected and courageous things, given the parameters of their life and times. These are folk who quietly believe in God, without presumption or fanfare, accepting his will and trying to live in ways that are consistent with his character. In doing so (and in being so), Ruth, Naomi, and Boaz speak to our hearts in a way that perhaps a Joshua, David, or Moses are unable to. And for that, *ḥesed* becomes real.

Journeys of Naomi and Ruth

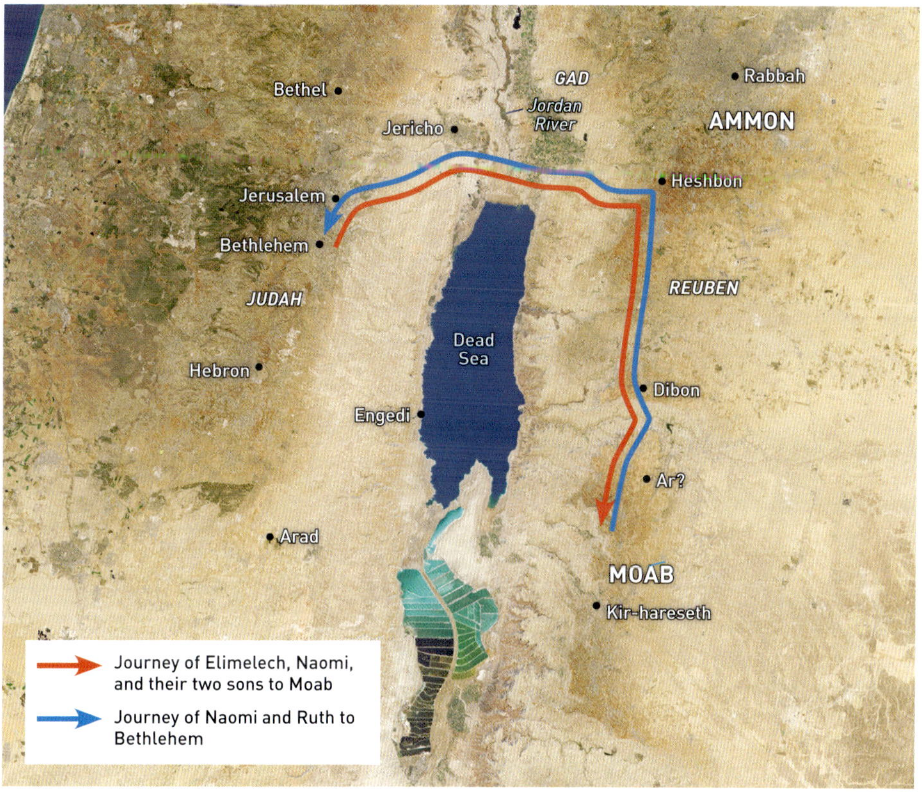

Themes in the Story of Ruth

When the world goes crazy, God always preserves a remnant of faithful people.

The opening phrase of the story of Ruth places its events "in the days when the judges ruled" (Ruth 1:1). This takes us to the biblical book of Judges, which ends with this statement: "In those days there was no king in Israel. Everyone did what was right in his own eyes" (Judg. 21:25). This was a turbulent time when temptations and expediencies pulled peoples' hearts in every direction. In the midst of it all we see Naomi and Boaz, with Ruth the foreigner, together forming a faithful remnant, what today we might call a minority, who still strives to follow God.

The theme that God preserves a faithful remnant is found throughout the Bible, with the promise that no matter the distress, his people will be restored (e.g., 2 Kings 19:4, 31; Ezra 9:8; Isa. 10:21; Jer. 23:3; Rom. 11:5). The story of Ruth provides a wonderful example of what a faithful remnant can be.

Bad things sometimes happen to good people.

We don't need the Bible to tell us this, although throughout the Bible—a book that doesn't pull any punches—we hear the desperate and often silent cry "Why?!" Sometimes the Bible attributes fractured lives and broken societies to the judgment of God, brought on by peoples' persistent transgressions and sin. But not always. Sometimes the Bible just recognizes the dilemma and lets us hear the pain of the human heart (Pss. 39; 42; 88).

Often we read in the Old Testament that God, as a way of waking his people up, takes away the fertility of the land on which Israel lives (Lev. 26:19–20; Deut. 11:13–17; 28:15–68; Isa. 24:1–23; 33:9; Ezek. 14:13). We note C. S. Lewis's observation that "pain insists on being attended to"; it is God's "megaphone to rouse a deaf world."[1] But at the same time, famine in the land of ancient Israel, a land that is especially susceptible to poor rainfall anyway, sometimes happens for no apparent reason other than the natural vagaries of climate. And so Naomi, already away from her homeland and the circle of relatives in which she finds security, loses her husband and sons, leaving her bereft of provision and legal protection. She sees her misfortune as something that is God-given (Ruth 1:20–21). But are we to think that God *causes* her miserable situation or just allows it? The story doesn't say, and in that we recognize that when we are in the midst of distress, we, too, often don't know.

God wants everyone to follow him.

While we can glory in the deeds of people like Moses, David, or the apostle Paul, the Bible is chock-full of examples of how God also guides the feet of the rest of us. Psalm 139, a psalm of David, reads as the voice of Everyone:

> *In your book were written, every one of them,*
> *the days that were formed for me,*
> *when as yet there was none of them. (Psalm 139:16)*

It is true that most of the Bible's stories focus on the descendants of Jacob. But here we see Boaz, an Israelite, marrying Ruth the Moabite, with God blessing the union. Ruth confesses her belief in God and everything that this entails when she refuses to leave Naomi and fully immerses herself in the Torah-infused world of Israel (Ruth 1:16–17). The apostle Paul calls such conversions "circumcision of the heart, by the Spirit" (Rom. 2:29 NIV), and he teaches that God's bottom-line plan for everyone is belief in him (Eph. 2:11–22).

God wants people to care for others, especially those who are less fortunate or in need.

The instruction that people should care for others, even those considered outsiders, penetrates all parts of the Bible (Deut. 10:18–19; Jer. 7:5–7; 22:3; Matt. 25:34–40; 1 Peter 5:7). This is especially true for people of means who are told to provide for the vulnerable in society, including widows (like Naomi and Ruth) and orphans and foreigners (again, Ruth). Rather than simply stating this obligation as some parts of the Bible do, like the Law and the exhortations of the prophets, the book of Ruth *shows* what it's all about. In Ruth's story, we see honor and blessing all wrapped up in *ḥesed*, loyalty, with Boaz labeled "a worthy man" (Ruth 2:1) and Ruth "a worthy woman" (Ruth 3:11). As the events unfold, we see people acting in ways that they are supposed to act under the umbrella of a God-fearing society, the benefits and drawbacks of patriarchy notwithstanding.

God works through the actions of his people, no matter whether the actions are wise, conniving, or left to happenstance.

Like many stories in the Bible, God is active but off-stage, with the fingerprints of providence everywhere. Once back in Bethlehem, Naomi is a stay-at-home activist (she has been termed "first among the Managerial

Women … the subtlest and most loving schemer of them all"[2]). Boaz, her relative, is the insightful landowner, an overseer who is quick to act. And then we have faithful, courageous Ruth, far from home yet exactly in the right place, bringing Naomi and Boaz together in a marvelous resolution.

This is a story of redemption, so God must be involved. We can argue that he is the main character in every Bible story, even though the only verses in the book of Ruth where the narrator attributes specific actions to him are 1:6 and 4:13 where the Lord makes the land and people fruitful (these are the blessings of creation). There are no prayers, oracles, prophets, sacrifices, or priests in the story; just people doing the right thing at the right time—though a few others, all minor characters, do the wrong thing in contrast. So we see God working through the good graces of his people; a more sophisticated theological understanding would be that he gives people their good graces to begin with.

We also see that God works through what we sometimes call happenstance: "And [Ruth] *happened* to come to the part of the field belonging to Boaz" (Ruth 2:3, emphasis added). This is a testimony to the providential will of God if there ever was one. James, not limiting the manner in which God's grace appears, says it this way: "Every good gift and every perfect gift is from above, coming down from the Father of lights" (James 1:17).

Events in the Story of Ruth

Scene 1: Emptiness RUTH 1:1–22

A famine in Bethlehem prompts Elimelech, Naomi, and their two sons, Mahlon and Chilion, to move to Moab. The sons marry Moabite women, Orpah and Ruth. After Naomi's husband and sons die, she returns to Bethlehem, accompanied by Ruth.

In the opening line of the first scene, famine strikes Bethlehem, a town with a name that, ironically, means "the house of bread." While never a large city, Bethlehem has ample land suitable for orchards and grain fields nearby, though not sufficient to quell hungry tummies when the rains fail. Living conditions at the time of the story are hand to mouth anyway, with no structures outside the local community to provide aid. The result is that Bethlehem's residents are wholly dependent on the annual harvest for food (indeed, this has been the situation for most of the people in the history of the world, most of the time).

Because of famine, Elimelech decides to move his family from Bethlehem to Moab, a place outside the borders of Israel. The story gives no indication that this decision is due to a lack of faith in God's ability to provide. Rather, it seems to be a simple choice of expediency based on what is best for his family, given the situation at hand. The high tableland of Moab, east of the Dead Sea, is within sight of Bethlehem, and likely Elimelech has seen ample rainclouds there when the skies above his Bethlehem home remained blue.

The fertile fields of Moab, here sharing crops of wheat and olives

The meaning of personal names often plays a role in biblical stories, either directly, with the name explained as a note in the narrative (e.g., Gen. 4:1; 17:5; 29:32–33:24; 1 Sam. 1:20), or indirectly, as in the book of Ruth, with actions depicting the meaning of the name.

- Elimelech = "God is king." This is an appropriate name for an ancestor of King David.
- Naomi = "pleasant." Naomi changes her identity to Mara = "bitter," reflecting her misfortune.
- Ruth = possibly "companion" or "satisfied." The meaning of Ruth's name is not certain, but either option works well in the story.

- Mahlon = "sickly" and Chilion = "weakly." These might be nicknames, since the boys die too soon. (It's hard to believe that a mom would give her boys such names at birth!)
- Boaz = possibly "quickness" or "alacrity." The meaning of Boaz's name is also uncertain, but both possibilities appropriately reflect his eagerness to help.
- Obed = "one who serves." This grandson of Naomi will provide for her in her old age.

According to the norms of patriarchy, Ruth and Orpah should both have stayed in Moab after they became widows, returning to their own father's house for support and perhaps finding another husband among their own people as well. But Naomi insists that they return to their "mother's house" (Ruth 1:8). The distinction is important. The term "mother's house" refers primarily to the social space within the physical confines of a family compound that served to strengthen the personhood of women living in a patriarchal society. Naomi doesn't just say "Go back home" but rather "Return to the people who can best care for you—and the Lord will bless you!" On the face of it, Orpah's choice to remain in Moab is the logical and sensible one; Ruth's is courageous, risky, and, in a society as conservative as was early Israel, countercultural. Ruth's loyalty to Naomi, but also to her husband who died without an heir, both foreigners to her family, is stronger than her loyalty to her own people. For her part, Naomi doesn't want her daughters-in-law to participate in her cursed life as she returns to whatever might remain for her back home (Ruth 1:12–13).

We usually praise Ruth for leaving her birth home to follow Naomi, without considering the severity of what awaits her. Already she has done something outside normal cultural expectations by marrying a foreigner (what kind of father would have allowed *that* in the day? cf. Judg. 14:3). Now Ruth is leaving behind everything that has forged her identity and that she calls home, going off to live in a small town in another land where she has never been, to live out her life with an older woman who does not share her family's blood and has become disillusioned with her own life's turn, knowing she will probably never return. What kind of woman does this? And how is this supposed to work out well for her? Abraham had done something similar, except that he had heard the call of God (Gen. 12:1–3); Ruth hasn't, at least in the same dramatic way. Her confession is sincere, earnest, pleading, yet betrays her innocence about where she is going. "Your people shall be my people, and your God my God" (Ruth 1:16), Ruth says, and this is her only reference to the Israelite deity in the story. In it, Ruth uses the generic name for God, *Elohim*, as an awakening conscience would, while throughout the rest of the story Naomi and Boaz, as Israelites, use God's revealed name Yahweh (the LORD). While admiring Ruth's courageous vision and faith, we are left to ponder just how she might have come to this point in her life.

The passage of time in rural Israelite villages was reckoned in the most practical way possible, by the times of planting and harvesting that mark the change of seasons (Lev. 26:4–5; Num. 13:20; Judg. 15:1; 2 Sam. 21:9–10; Amos 7:1). The timing of these activities varied from place to place and year by year, with famine upsetting the overall rhythm. And so the opening scene of Ruth's story closes with a bit of foreshadowing: "They came to Bethlehem at the beginning of barley harvest" (Ruth 1:22), that is, at the beginning of spring.

Scene 2: Hope RUTH 2:1–23

To provide for herself and Naomi, Ruth gleans grain in the fields of Boaz, a well-positioned relative of her late husband. Boaz shows favor to Ruth by allowing her to work in the fields alongside his own people.

When the second scene opens, Naomi and Ruth are still living under the very real consequences of famine: they need something to eat. An initial solution sees them resort to gleaning. As a social-security system, the Torah provisions of Leviticus 19:9–10 and Deuteronomy 24:19 instruct landowners to leave standing grain around the edges of their fields or leave unpicked grapes in their vineyards, so that those who are disadvantaged can glean something to eat. As she gleans, Ruth "happens" to come to the field of Boaz (Ruth 2:3). Showing boldness, desperation, or both, Ruth asks the foreman if she can not only glean but also reap close to Boaz's regular workers where she can find both provision and protection (Ruth 2:7–9). Admiring Ruth's character and her devotion to Naomi, Boaz allows this and then welcomes her to eat with him and the reapers, an indication that she, a foreigner, is being accepted into the support networks of Bethlehem (Ruth 2:11–12, 14). As the story progresses, the narrator is careful to show Ruth's transition from "the young Moabite woman, who came back with Naomi from the country of Moab" (a foreigner; Ruth 2:6) to "my daughter" (a dependent; Ruth 2:8; 3:1, 10) to "a worthy woman" (a full participant in the life of Bethlehem; Ruth 3:11).

Naomi meanwhile plays the role of the mother, planning what she can control within the boundaries and expectations of the day to provide a future for herself and for Ruth. Perhaps we would have liked Naomi to have told Ruth to go to the field of Boaz straight away or for Boaz to have noticed that "the whole town was stirred because of them" (Ruth 1:19) and volunteered to help up front. But the encounter of Ruth and Boaz was, we might say, fortuitous (Ruth 2:3), something the story clearly suggests is by the hand of God.

Ruth Gleaning in the Fields (James Tissot, c. 1896-1902)

When the narrator introduces Boaz, he properly identifies him with genealogical language: Boaz is a relative of Naomi on her husband's side from the clan of Elimelech (Ruth 2:1; 3:2). Identifying someone by their genealogical address was typical in the biblical world (e.g., 1 Sam 9:1; Luke 2:36). The Hebrew term *moda'*, translated here as "relative" (sometimes as "kinsman"), is a generic term and from it we cannot know what the actual blood tie of Boaz to Elimelech is.

More significantly, Boaz is also identified as an *ish gibor hayil*. The literal translation is "a mighty man," leaving the context to determine mighty in what way. Translators usually understand Boaz to have been mighty in either wealth or virtue, although the term can also mean mighty in battle. English translations vary: "a man of standing" (NIV); "a man of great wealth" (NKJV and NASB); "a mighty man of wealth" (KJV); "a prominent man of noble character" (CSB); and "a worthy man" (ESV), with the older translations focusing on Boaz's wealth and the more recent ones emphasizing his character. While the story shows that Boaz is mighty in both, the emphasis is not on his wealth per se but how he uses it in virtuous ways.

Depiction of the ark of the covenant with cherubim

Ruth may not be mighty in the sense that Boaz is in society, but her character and deeds in the story are commanding, earning her the admiration of mighty Boaz: "The LORD repay you for what you have done, and a full reward be given you by the LORD, the God of Israel, under whose wings you have come to take refuge!" (Ruth 2:12). The poetic idiom of taking refuge under the wings of a deity is common in the language and art of the ancient Near East (cf. Deut. 32:11; Pss. 17:8; 36:7; 57:1; 61:4; 63:7; 91:4; Mal. 4:2). For instance, in Egypt several deities were depicted as birds with wings outstretched to shield people underneath, most notably the falcon-god Horus protecting Pharaoh. In Israel, the cover of the ark of the covenant was adorned with cherubim whose wings were "spread out

. . . overshadowing the mercy seat" (Ex. 25:20). The deity with outstretched wings of whom Boaz speaks is "the LORD, the God of Israel" under whom Ruth has taken refuge. Here Boaz acknowledges Ruth's commitment to follow Naomi, filling in the identity of the God whom she has also chosen to follow.

Naomi calls Boaz her *go'el*, a word rendered in English as "redeemer" or sometimes "kinsman-redeemer" (Ruth 2:20). This term is used in a variety of ways in the Old Testament, initially having to do with a person using their means or influence to help those of their in-group who are less fortunate. It then became a very powerful idiom for describing the actions of God. The kinsman-redeemer:

- bought back clan property (Lev. 25:25–30; Jer. 32:1–15);
- bought clan members out of slavery (Lev. 25:47–55);
- took vengeance on someone who killed a clan member (Num. 35:12–27); and
- assisted clan members in lawsuits or complaints to see that justice was done (Ps. 119:154; Prov. 23:10–11; Jer. 50:34).

At this point in the story of Ruth, Boaz the redeemer helps Ruth and Naomi get something to eat; later it will be much more.

Scene 3: Promise RUTH 3:1–18

Naomi devises a plan so that both she and Ruth will regain enough standing in Bethlehem to be able to live securely. After a nighttime rendezvous with Ruth at the threshing floor, Boaz decides to act as a redeemer and provide security for her and Naomi.

Because a good harvest in ancient Israel is equivalent to having a full bank account today, harvest time was a time of opportunity for settling debts and entering into new economic and social relationships. It is also an appropriate time for Naomi to secure her and Ruth's future through Boaz. Naomi wants to find a permanent home where she and Ruth will be well provided for, but her plan that Ruth lie down next to Boaz at the threshing floor seems, on the face of it, to be a bit scandalous. We don't know enough about the customs of the day to know if a chaste woman going to the threshing floor at night was even culturally possible, let alone exceptional; it could have been either given Boaz's hushed concern (Ruth 3:14).

Threshing floors were wide areas of open-air bedrock, often on the tops of hills exposed to the breeze. The grain fields filled valley floors below. After the grain was harvested by cutting the stalks in the field, it was taken to the threshing floor. There the grain was threshed by pulling a wooden sledge with stone teeth over it, knocking the heads of grain from the stalks. The farmer then tossed the entire mass into the air with a large wooden winnowing fork so that the wind could blow away the chaff, leaving the heavier heads of grain behind. These were communal areas, with each family's harvested grain piled on a different section of the threshing floor. A prudent farmer would sleep next to his own harvest each night until his grain could be threshed, collected, and bagged, lest his enterprising neighbor abscond with part of his crop. (These practices persisted in the Middle East up until the introduction of gasoline-powered farming equipment in modern times.)

A threshing floor near Bethlehem, protected by a stone wall

Slumbering Boaz awakes on the threshing floor, startled to find Ruth sleeping near his feet! Ruth takes the initiative: "Spread your wings [literally the wide, flappy edge of a cloak] over your servant, for you are a redeemer" (Ruth 3:9). Covering a woman with the corner of one's cloak, its "wings," was understood to be a symbol of intended marriage in the ancient Near East. Ruth seems to be the one proposing to Boaz, even though she is younger, a foreigner, a field-worker, and, of course, a *she*.[3] In any case, Ruth's primary motive is to find a way for Naomi to be restored. For Ruth, that marriage ends up being part of the arrangement seems to be the means rather than the end. Whatever does or doesn't happen as Ruth lays at Boaz's feet—the Hebrew term for feet, *regel*, can mean anything from the waist down, and Boaz had drunk to good spirits the evening before (Ruth 3:7)—the whole scene is fraught with danger and is rather scandalous, even if she didn't "do" anything.[4] Clearly there is some double entendre the way the story is told, and we are at a rather delicate moment in the action (or lack of action as the case may be). Based on Boaz's reaction, most (but not all) commentators embrace the virtue of the couple and understand the night to have been a chaste encounter. Because the threshing floor is a public place, Boaz is rightly concerned what others might think (honor once lost is almost impossible to regain), so he is careful to send Ruth away before dawn.

By reminding Boaz that he is Naomi's redeemer, Ruth fully confesses that as Naomi's *daughter* she is part of a Bethlehem family and not just an out-of-place daughter-in-law. When Boaz sees that Ruth is placing Naomi's needs above her own, he calls her an *eshet hayil*, "a worthy woman" or "a woman of noble character" (Ruth 3:11). This is the equivalent of his identity, revealed earlier in the story, as "a worthy man," sometimes rendered "a prominent man of noble character" (Ruth 2:1). *Eshet hayil* is the same phrase used in the book of Proverbs to describe the woman of Proverbs 31:10–31. In the Hebrew Bible the book of Ruth is placed immediately after the book of Proverbs, allowing the reader to see by specific actions what this woman of worth can be.

Boaz knows that the closest male relative to someone in trouble carries the responsibility of serving as their redeemer. This closest relative is mentioned in the narrative but, as is the case for many minor characters in the Bible, he is not named. By remaining anonymous, he avoids being forever remembered for the shame of acting only for his own interests. At the same time, he becomes a foil that heightens the noble qualities of Boaz in the narrative flow.

Boaz knows the role of the redeemer and wants to be the one to restore Naomi to fullness, life the way it's supposed to be. All the clues in the story so far point toward marriage as being a part of what it will mean for Boaz to redeem both Ruth and Naomi, although we don't find out if this will be part of the solution until the last scene. In the meantime, both Boaz and Ruth act with the valor that their names imply. When Ruth returns to Naomi after her nighttime encounter, she and Naomi are already changed women, even though they don't know yet exactly what will happen. The scene closes with the promise that Boaz will make things right.

Scene 4: Restoration RUTH 4:1–22

Boaz steps in to redeem Naomi's land and marry Ruth, then counts their children and the wealth derived from the land as belonging to the line of Naomi's late husband. Naomi's life is restored, and she becomes an ancestor of king David.

The culminating scene in the story of Ruth takes place within Bethlehem's city gate. In ancient Israel the city gate was the location of legal decisions. Called to adjudicate or witness a formal decision, the town's elders met in one of the chambers that composed the gate complex, in full view of all interested parties (there were no backroom deals). The goal was to find a resolution that would satisfy everyone. Remains of Israelite Bethlehem, including its gate, likely lie beneath the Church of the Nativity and Manger Square in the heart of the modern city and have not been uncovered by archaeologists. However, gate complexes have been excavated in other Israelite cities, which help us picture the setting.

Outer gate of the Israelite city of Dan

The two driving concerns for an ancient Israelite were that their family line continue and that their ancestral land remain in the family. Descendants and land provided the best recourse for protection and security in old age. We already know that Naomi's bloodline has essentially ended (Ruth 1:11–13); now we see that she also has no recourse to live off her dead husband's property and so is forced to sell it for whatever she can get (Ruth 4:3). We are not told why: perhaps it has laid fallow too long, and Naomi lacks the means to bring it back into productivity. Perhaps a squatter (the nearer kinsman?) has taken the land during her lengthy absence in Moab and the only means she has of evicting him is selling it out from under him—or hoping that he will be forced to fess up and buy it from her. In any case, lacking access to the food source derived from Elimelech's land, Naomi remains destitute, and she and Ruth are likely to fall into debt-slavery. As a solution, Naomi chooses to sell the land for whatever one-time gain she can get. Boaz steps in to restore her rights, knowing that the process requires some customary legal details.

The nearer kinsman, who is not named, is happy enough to buy the land and add it to his own estate, which will then be inherited by his own children. But Boaz tells him that the land and the lady come together. If the nearer kinsman marries Ruth, her children by him will inherit the land, giving him only temporary gain and opening his two sets of sons to the real possibility of fighting over his estate. This he chooses to avoid.

Many scholars see this episode as an example of levirate marriage, a legal provision in ancient Israel in which a man receives his dead brother's property and manages it for the widow. If the widow has no male heirs, then he is obligated to marry her to raise up heirs so that the land will remain in the bloodline of his dead brother (Deut. 25:5–10). Even though the nearer kinsman is not Elimelech's brother, this story adheres to the principle of levirate marriage, providing an example of how the instructions of Torah are flexible enough to apply to analogous situations. The overarching goal of Torah, in any case, is to teach Israelites how to live wisely, aligned with the character of God, in their own circumstances of life. We should note that the verb "redeem" (*ga'al*), from which the term "redeemer" (*go'el*) is derived, does not appear in the laws of levirate marriage in Deuteronomy 25 but is found in the laws of redemption of land and freedom of debt-slaves, both of which are also at play in the story (Lev. 25:25–28, 47–50).

The deal at the city gate between Boaz and the nearer kinsman is sealed not with a handshake but with a shoe! The note in Ruth 4:7 that "in former times" legal matters were ratified by the giving of a sandal is a glimpse into a specific aspect of customary law in ancient Israel. The Bible includes other instances of legal customs or ordinances that develop due to specific circumstances or to fit local needs (Num. 36:1–12; 1 Sam. 30:23–25; Jer. 34:8–11). None of these customs are specifically covered in the original legal material of the Pentateuch. Because the word *Torah*, usually translated as "law," means "instruction," many scholars have concluded that the legal material of the Pentateuch is not so much a complete code of jurisprudence as it is instructions for ethical and moral standards for how Israel should behave as a community. The succinct injunction of Leviticus 19:15–18—"You shall do no injustice in court.... But you shall love your neighbor as yourself"—is illustrated in the specific case of Naomi and Ruth by the actions of Boaz.

The legal proceedings at the Bethlehem gate do not treat Ruth like merchandise but are a ratification, according to the customs and expectations of the day, legitimizing the relationship status that she and Boaz both want and had agreed upon the prior night. The sentence "Also Ruth the Moabite, the widow of Mahlon, I have bought (*qaḥnah*) to be my wife" (Ruth 4:10) uses the same verb that Eve speaks upon bearing her firstborn son, Cain: "I have gotten [bought] a man with the help of the Lord" (Gen. 4:1). We should subsume whatever economic ramifications this term might carry to its primary sense of entering into a mutually productive relationship. The witnesses to the legal proceeding bless Ruth by likening her to the matriarchs Rachel and Leah, who "built up the house of Israel" (Ruth 4:11; cf. Gen. 29:15–30:24).

Later, the women of Bethlehem who gasped at the destitute fate of Naomi when she first returned home rejoice with her when Ruth and Boaz bear a son. Here the blessings are directed to Naomi rather than to the beaming couple, since in the end it is she, not Ruth, who is redeemed: "[Boaz] shall be to you a restorer of life and a nourisher of your old age" (Ruth. 4:15). In a tender glimpse into the provide-and-protect values of small-village communal Israel, it is the women of Bethlehem who give the baby Obed his name. Aptly named Obed, "the one who serves," is counted as belonging to Naomi (Ruth 4:16–17). As the episode ends, we discover that this has not been Ruth's story at all, but Naomi's.

Added to the end of the story is a genealogy showing that David and his royal line will descend from Ruth and Boaz, the kind of virtuous, caring people whom monarchs should also strive to be (Ruth 4:18–22). In the Bible, genealogies are usually partial in the sense that not every name or every generation is (or needs to be) mentioned. This genealogy, also abbreviated, begins with Perez, son of the patriarch Judah, to indicate that David descends from Judah. This gives the future king of Israel deep roots. But a troubling story in Genesis 38 reveals that Perez was born of Judah's incestuous relationship with his daughter Tamar. Enter the story of Naomi, Ruth, and Boaz; their behavior overshadows, and maybe even erases, Judah's questionable reputation, cleaning up the way for the royal Davidic line to unfold with virtue, courage, and righteousness. Ruth and Boaz die content, yet never knowing that their great grandson will become the greatest king of Israel or that from their line an even greater king, Jesus, will someday descend (Matt. 1:5–6, 16).

A view of Bethlehem at sunset from an olive grove east of the village

RUTH IN LATER WRITINGS

- Ruth and Boaz are mentioned elsewhere in the Bible only in genealogical lists, primarily as ancestors of Jesus (1 Chron. 2:11–12; Matt. 1:5; Luke 3:32).

- Because the story of Ruth is so beautiful, she and Boaz become types, or examples, of piety and chaste behavior, universally praised by Jewish and Christian commentators alike. For Christians, Ruth is a type of Mary, an unmarried woman who finds favor with God (Luke 1:26–28) and then bears a son in the line of David. Boaz the redeemer is a type of Christ, putting the needs of others above his own.

- For Jews, the story of Ruth teaches how great is the reward of those who do deeds of *ḥesed*, kindness.[5] The book of Ruth is also one of the five books, or scrolls, of the Hebrew Bible which since the Middle Ages have been linked to the annual Jewish festivals. Ruth is read during the Feast of Weeks (*Shavuot*, or Pentecost) marking the wheat harvest in the land of Israel (early June). This link is natural since it is during the barley and wheat harvests that the events in the story take place. But it also provides a yearly reminder of the gracious provision we all receive, whether it be through natural means such as rainfall and harvest (Gen. 8:22; Ps. 65:9–13) or the caring acts of people who align their lives with the righteous character of God.

Study Questions

1. What cultural challenges do modern readers face as they study Bible stories about people living in times and places so very different from their own? As a student of Scripture, what helps you think through ancient stories like Ruth's?

2. Famine was a particularly feared prospect in the biblical world. What might be an equivalent disaster in prosperous, industrialized societies today?

3. Consider the main characters: Naomi, Ruth, and Boaz. What does each have? What does each need? What are their most noble characteristics? How does each provide for themselves and for others?

4. What would an *ish gibor hayil* ("man of noble character") and an *eshet hayil* ("woman of noble character") look like today?

5. How would you describe the providential will of God? How is his will evident in the story of Ruth?

6. What does Boaz do to be Naomi's *go'el* ("kinsman-redeemer")? How does this foreshadow or anticipate the actions of Jesus?

Chapter 4 Notes

1 C. S. Lewis, *The Problem of Pain* (MacMillan, 1962), 93.
2 Maurice Samuel, *Certain People of the Book* (Union of American Hebrew Congregations, 1955), 107.
3 David Instone-Brewer, Divorce and Remarriage in the Bible: The Social and Literary Context (Eerdmans, 2002), 1–2n2.
4 For a summary, see Daniel I. Block, "Ruth 1: Book of," in *Dictionary of the Old Testament: Wisdom, Poetry and Writings,* eds. Tremper Longman III and Peter Enns (IVP Academic, 2008), 682.
5 *Ruth Rabbah,* 2:14.

Chapter 4 Images

Ruth and Naomi by P. H. Calderon, 1886
Journeys of Ruth and Naomi; satellite map courtesy of NASA
Moab (Paul H. Wright)
Ruth Gleaning in the Fields by James Tissot, c. 1896–1902, The Jewish Museum
Ark (P Maxwell Photography/Shutterstock)
Threshing floor (Paul H. Wright)
Tel Dan gate (Alla Khananashvili/Shutterstock)
Bethlehem (John Theodor/Bethlehem)

Chapter 5

THE STORY OF DAVID AND GOLIATH

1 Samuel 17

DAVID VERSUS GOLIATH. It's a phrase that's become an idiom. Popular culture reduces the story to a struggle of the little guy triumphing over the big guy, the corner store sticking it to the corporation, the average Joe beating city hall. But the story is about more, much more.

David's encounter with Goliath is a pivotal episode at the midpoint of the book of 1 Samuel. It's a tightly crafted narrative recounting a single encounter of Israel against the Philistines. In it, a strapping young fellow we meet in the prior chapter of 1 Samuel, David-of-unlikely-beginnings, overcomes not only a superior foe in the uncouth giant but also his own king, the hopelessly inadequate Saul. The main plotline in the book of 1 Samuel centers on the search for effective leadership in early Israel, culminating in the rise of David, "a man after [God's] own heart" (1 Sam. 13:14).

As the book opens, leadership is vested in the high priest Eli. God rejects Eli and his corrupt sons for Samuel, whose servant heart listens (1 Sam. 3:10). Samuel functions as Israel's priest, prophet, and judge. But as he ages, the Israelites demand a king so "that we also may be like all the nations, and that our king may judge us and go out before us and fight our battles" (1 Sam. 8:20; cf. Ezek. 20:32). Samuel acquiesces, anointing Saul who, for a while, shows great promise. But eventually Saul self-destructs. Proving himself disqualified for kingship, his disobedience to God spins out in ineffective leadership. In the words of Josephus, "Saul had made God his enemy."[1] It's not a good place to end up.

Under God's direction, Samuel anoints a new king, David, from a different tribe and family line. As readers, we know about this anointing; Saul, in the storyline, has no idea that David, a youngster whom he chooses to soothe his foul moods, will grow up to be the man who replaces him. As the plot of the first half of the book of 1 Samuel twists around Israel's dodgy chances of survival in the face of growing Philistine pressure, we see God's hand preparing the heart of a faithful lad who will rise to plant Israel firmly in their land.

David versus Goliath is not just a Bible story recounting part of this struggle. It is also a historical event, and here we need to find additional context. The Philistines, with Goliath as their champion at the moment, are remnants of the Mycenean kingdom that was collapsing in a land that later becomes part of Greece. Jeremiah 47:4 and Amos 9:7 pinpoint their homeland as Caphtor, which most scholars identify as the island

Philistine Migration

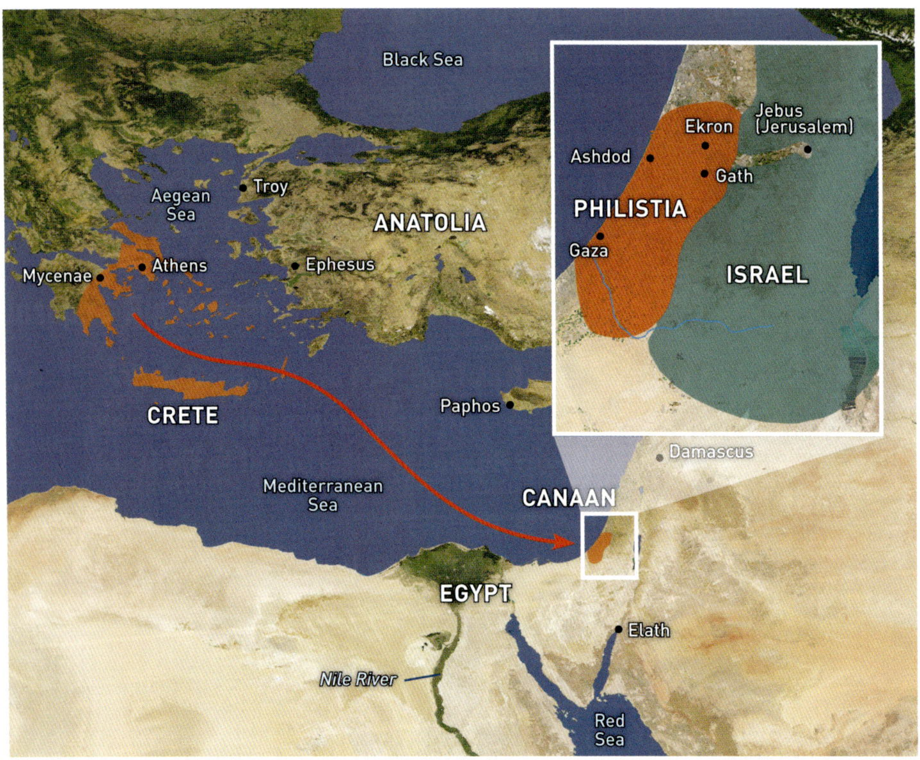

of Crete. Texts from ancient Egypt call the Philistines *Peleshet*, one of several "Sea Peoples" (to use Egyptian terminology) who settled along the coast of Canaan in the thirteenth century BC and challenged both Egyptian and Canaanite interests there. Because the Israelites are also moving in under Joshua at about the same time, although entering from the opposite direction, the stage is set for a showdown of just who will control what in Canaan.

A philistine jug used to strain liquids

Archaeological evidence shows the Philistines to have been a very sophisticated people, with high culture, fine art, advanced weaponry, and clear ties to the Aegean. They settled on a very profitable part of Canaan, the coastal plain, where they came to control international commerce and trade. Large urban centers dominated by the Philistines spread throughout the area, functioning together in a loose confederation of shared power. Gath, home of Goliath, was one of these cities, and every indication is that however much we want to picture Goliath as an uncouth lout, his kinsfolk carried themselves in ways that looked rather attractive to their new neighbors. The Philistines were Indo-Europeans, not Semites, so they were very different from the Canaanites and Israelites in language, religion, social structure, and material culture. But like new arrivals everywhere, the Philistines came to merge with the locals over time. (The eastern seaboard of the Mediterranean, a busy corridor, has always been a melting pot of people coming and going). For Israel, a new people themselves, assimilating to other ideas about God and what makes for a good life was a persistent temptation, prompting the age-old question, "Just how different does God want us to be?"

The Philistine military threat loomed large as Israel sought to secure their home in the same land. (To be fair, if we had Philistine texts from the same time, we would probably read that they felt just as threatened by Israel as Israel was by them.) On the kingdom level, the issues were security and economic growth. On the personal level, we might call these needs protection and provision. These concerns seem to be universals; the relevant question for us today might be, "How open am I to the will of God in determining what security and provision should look like in situations that I face?" In any case, based on the biblical record and archaeological data, it is clear that throughout the period of Israel's settlement, the Philistines sought to check and hinder Israel's emerging kingdom by slow attrition and attacking its power centers.[2] Here is the sequence recorded in the Bible:

- **Judges 13:1–16:31** An initial Philistine incursion pushes eastward from the coast toward the Israelite hill country, filling an intermediate lowland zone called the Valley of Sorek west of Jerusalem (Judg. 16:4). This is the arena of Samson, whose exploits in checking the Philistine advance are challenged by his own people, who warn, "Do you not know that the Philistines are rulers over us? What then is this that you have done to us?" (Judg. 15:11; cf. Judg. 14:4). Samson's feats are heroic (well, most of them), but after he dies, the situation remains a stalemate, with Israel and the Philistines staring each other down.

- **1 Samuel 4:1–11** The Philistines defeat Israel in battle between Ebenezer and Aphek, at a point where the northeastern corner of Philistine control touches the area of Israelite settlement in the orb of Shiloh, Israel's religious and political capital. The Philistines capture the ark of the covenant in the process, holding it hostage deep in Philistine territory. Archaeological evidence shows that Shiloh was destroyed at the same time, likely in a follow-up campaign.

- **1 Samuel 7:7–11** After the destruction of Shiloh, the center of Israel's leadership moves to the vicinity of Samuel's family hometown of Ramah, midway between Shiloh and Jerusalem. To counter, the Philistines make a frontal attack on Mizpeh, a nearby Israelite town on a strategic crossroads in that region. Panicked by God-induced thunder, the Philistines flee.

- **1 Samuel 13:2–14:23** Apparently seeking to test the resolve of Israel's new king, Saul, the Philistines press deeper into Israelite territory, this time to Michmash overlooking the Jordan Valley. In doing so, they surround Saul's hometown of Gibeah—which he made Israel's capital—on three sides. But in a time that demands decisive action, Saul is wholly ineffective, leaving his son Jonathan to start an ambush that drives the Philistines out of Israelite territory.

Enter Goliath. Not willing to risk another head-on assault, the Philistines decide to do an end-around, approaching the Israelite center of power from the southwest, confident that this time they will succeed. As for the Israelite response, how are they supposed to win this battle when their king is afraid? But God has a plan. Enter David.

Themes in the Story of David and Goliath

God desires sustained, effective leadership for his people.

David has it; Saul doesn't. Throughout the Bible, we see that God raises up leaders to guide, teach, or govern his people or to save them from harm. Often these are individuals called to specific situations, and only occasionally are the Israelites able to sustain effective leadership over multiple generations. Leadership is certainly spotty throughout the time of the judges, the centuries leading up to the rise of David. But even within David's kingdom—and here the royal line lasts for three hundred years—half of the kings are rascals, and the priesthood doesn't fare much better (Ezek. 34:1–31). Yet when Israel's leaders are upright and seek to govern by principles that reflect God's character, the people prosper. The Bible's most powerful image of effective leadership is the shepherd, a person who tends the flock under his care 24/7. The skills necessary to be a good shepherd include courage, resourcefulness, persistence, strength, foresight, willingness to take risks for others, and the ability to place the needs of the sheep above his, or her, own. Abraham, Moses, and David are all shepherds long before God calls them to "shepherd … his people" (Ps. 78:71). So it is with all God's people: Jesus "the good shepherd" (John 10:11, 14) commissions Peter to "tend my sheep," a charge for us as well (John 21:16).

God often chooses the weak over the strong.

We tend to expect people who are the most talented or who have access to the largest set of resources to accomplish the greatest things. But God expects all of us to use to its fullest whatever talent he has given us and to do so in ways that honor his character. The writers of the Bible recognize that even people whose innate abilities are, on the whole, rather average, are capable of doing great things. The apostle Paul puts it this way to the believers in Corinth:

> *Not many of you were wise according to worldly standards, not many were powerful, not many were of noble birth. But God chose what is foolish in the world to shame the wise; God chose what is weak in the world to shame the strong; God chose what is low and despised in the world, even things that are not, to bring to nothing things that are. (1 Cor. 1:26–28)*

The Old Testament is full of stories that illustrate the apostle's observation. Neither Joseph, Moses, Barak, Gideon, Jephthah, Hannah, Jeremiah, Amos, Esther, Mary, nor the boy Jesus who astonishes the teachers of Jerusalem is an individual from whom his or her contemporaries expect much—or, in some cases, think much of in the first place.[3] We can add the young shepherd boy David to this list.

God looks at the heart.

What *kind* of person pleases God? When we first meet Saul, we read that "there was not a man among the people of Israel more handsome than he. From his shoulders upward he was taller than any of the people" (1 Sam. 9:2). We are led to think that he stands head and shoulders above everyone else in other ways as well. But when Saul meets David, he—and then Goliath—look at the shepherd boy's appearance and disdain him as nothing more than a ruddy kid (1 Sam. 17:33, 42). Samuel, too, is at first mostly impressed by the physical prowess of David's older brothers and quickly has to be reminded that "the LORD looks on the heart" (1 Sam. 16:7). It is an ageless insight that must be learned by each generation, even David. In spite of a long litany of personal failings that the biblical writer doesn't hide, David remains "a man after [God's] own heart" throughout his life (1 Sam. 13:14).

The battle is the Lord's.

There is no greater guarantee of failure than excessive over-confidence, especially if that confidence is placed in our own skills, wisdom, and strength. There is no question that Goliath's Philistines, like Israel's other enemies that we meet in the Old Testament—armies led by Pharaoh (Ex. 5:2), the Assyrian Rabshakeh (2 Kings 18:19–25), Nebuchadnezzar (2 Kings 25:1–7), and a host of others throughout the ages—are more powerful that Israel, and all of them fell in the end. And we must not forget that the Bible shows us that Israel's own leaders, when they turn to self for sufficiency, also fail badly (e.g., the downfalls of kings Solomon and Ahab; 1 Kings 11:1–40; 22:1–40). This is another lesson that even David has to learn (2 Sam. 24:1–25). Characters such as these provide the counterpoint that emphasizes by negative example an even greater truth: God is the deciding power. "The LORD saves not with sword and spear. For the battle is the LORD's" (1 Sam. 17:47; cf. Ex. 14:10–14; 15:1–18; Josh. 1:6–7; 2 Chron. 14:10–12; Ps. 24:7–10).

The Anointing of David by Samuel (Félix-Joseph Barrias, 1842)

God chose the house of David to carry the messianic line.

The story of how God has provided the Messiah to save his people fills the pages of the Bible, from the beginning of Genesis to the end of Revelation. The Hebrew word for messiah, *mashiach*, means "anointed one." The term designates several types of individuals in the Old Testament who are anointed for special service on behalf of the people of Israel. These include priests like Aaron, prophets such as Isaiah, and kings like Saul and David of Israel but also King Cyrus the Persian. Of them, the writers of the Old Testament see David as the epitome of what an anointed one should be, while at the same time they look forward to an even greater Anointed One to come. That Messiah, as we see in the Gospels, is Jesus, the Christ (*xristos* is the Greek word for "anointed one"). Although the word *messiah* doesn't appear in the story of David and Goliath and we don't read of David's role as king until later in the biblical narrative, his triumph over Goliath sets the stage for the kind of anointed one he will be.

Events in the Story of David and Goliath

Goliath's Wager 1 SAMUEL 17:1–11

The Philistine army presses into the tribal territory of Judah. Their champion, Goliath, issues a challenge for any Israelite to fight him as proxy in one-on-one combat with the loser becoming a servant of the victor.

The story of David and Goliath begins, and then ends, with more geographical detail than we find in most other Bible stories. We read several specific place names—Socoh, Judah, Azekah, Ephes-dammim, Valley of Elah, Gath, Ekron and Shaaraim (1 Sam. 17:1–2, 52)—and something about the terrain where the Philistine and Israelite armies face off (1 Sam. 17:3). Because the narrator doesn't explain where these places are, we must assume that the original readers not only knew their location but also why they are significant enough to be mentioned at all. Places, like people, often play a role in Bible stories as events unfold. Specific place names give us, the reader, a sense of the urgency that Saul and David must feel as the Philistines once again appear on the horizon—and their relief as the enemy flees into the sunset. We know from the earlier chapters of 1 Samuel that the Philistines have already failed in attacking Saul's home base by the most direct route, from the west. Now they try to run wide right and come in from the southwest, an unexpected direction. The Philistines push the length of the Valley of Elah, a natural corridor connecting the Philistine coast to the Judean hill country through a zone of low foothills. By pressing beyond Azekah, the mid-point of the valley, to Socoh, a site that clearly belongs to Judah (1 Sam. 17:1), they force Saul's hand. For Israel, this is a clear and present danger (to borrow a modern phrase). If the Philistines can push into the hill country south of Saul's home base, they can easily gut the tribe of Judah. Moreover, the only Judean town that would then stand in their way of reaching Saul's capital home of Gibeah is Bethlehem. (Jerusalem, lying between Bethlehem and Gibeah, is not yet in Israelite hands.) This is an existential crisis, one that threatens Israel's very existence, with an additional threat to Saul's own home, not to mention his very life, on the line.

The broad portion of the Elah Valley, as seen from Khirbet Qeiyafa

The story of David and Goliath gives just enough topographical detail for us to locate the most likely spot of battle: "Saul and the men of Israel were gathered, and encamped in the Valley of Elah, and drew up in line of battle against the Philistines. And the Philistines stood on the mountain on the one side, and Israel stood on the mountain on the other side, with a valley between them" (1 Sam. 17:2–3). In the phrase "Valley of Elah," the Hebrew term for valley is *emeq*, which means "broad valley," and such the valley is for its entire length. However, the term for the valley that separates the two hills on which the opposing armies stand is *gai*, a

The Battle of David and Goliath

narrow valley with steep sides. Here it is best to look where the Valley of Elah pinches into a tight, steep gorge at the very edge of the hill country.[4] Having already given up the Judean foothills to the Philistines, Saul makes his stand at the base of the rugged Judean hill country, apparently hoping that by doing so he will keep the Philistines out of his heartland while not risking his forces in open terrain.

Goliath is from Gath, the large Philistine city plugging the western end of the Valley of Elah. In the eyes of Goliath, the entire valley is his. The Hebrew text of 1 Samuel 17 calls Goliath by name only twice: once when he first enters the scene and again when David first notices him (1 Sam. 17:4, 23). All other times (twenty-three in total), Goliath is referred to only as "the Philistine" or "the uncircumcised Philistine," labeling him, in Israelite eyes, as a lout. (In modern parlance, the adjective *philistine* describes a person who is uncouth.) A Philistine name similar to Goliath inscribed on a broken piece of pottery was found during excavations at Gath (Tel es-Safi).

Goliath is "six cubits and a span" in height, around nine feet (2.75 m) tall (1 Sam 17:4). By comparison, the tallest human officially on record was Robert Wadlow (1918–1940), the Alton Giant, at 8 feet 11.1 inches

(2.72 m). Some commentators suggest that Goliath had acromegaly, an abnormal condition of the pituitary gland that produces too much growth hormone and sometimes affects eyesight (if so, David would have had a clear-eyed advantage in combat). The Septuagint (the Greek translation of the Old Testament from the third century BC), one of the Dead Sea Scrolls, and Josephus all state that Goliath's height was four cubits and a span, about six and a half feet (1.98 m).[5] This still would have been considerably taller than his contemporaries, even Saul. The point is not so much Goliath's raw height but that he was gigantic. Twice the narrator calls Goliath a "champion," using the Hebrew term *ish habbenayim*, which means someone exceptional, different from everyone else (1 Sam. 17:4, 23).

Goliath's armor is typical of an Aegean warrior. Perhaps the reason it is described in such detail in the story is because it's unfamiliar and hence scary to the Israelite audience, something worth writing home about (1 Sam. 17:5–7). The Philistines have a monopoly on iron and iron sharpening, leaving Israel without access to proper weapons or protection (1 Sam. 13:20–22). Clearly the size and weight of Goliath's armor and armaments, made of both bronze and iron and weighing in excess of 80 pounds (36 kg), is meant to scare not just his exposed opponent but also anyone who hears about it. We know from archaeology and reliefs of Philistine warriors found in Egypt that the Philistines carried relatively small, round convex shields, apparently covered with leather, and one or two spears.[6] Philistine weapons found in excavations include tapered, double-edged sword blades 3.5 feet (1 m) long and a spearhead 4.7 inches (12 cm) long. Goliath's spearhead at 600 shekels (16 lbs; 7 kg) is larger (1 Sam 17:7).

The "Spartacus" headdress of the Philistine captives depicted here is characteristic of Philistine attire.

As the two armies face off, the Philistine champion makes a wager: "Choose a man for yourselves, and let him come down to me. If he is able to fight with me and kill me, then we will be your servants. But if I prevail against him and kill him, then you shall be our servants and serve us" (1 Sam. 17:8–9). One-on-one, winner-take-all challenges are attested in ancient Near Eastern and Greco-Roman literature, though not frequently. A battle of champions is a good way to save bloodshed. The phrase "in Ephes-dammim" is usually taken to refer to an unknown location where the Philistines set up camp (1 Sam. 17:1). But because Ephes-dammim means "without bloodshed," it may just be a note that no fighting had taken place prior to Goliath's challenge. Like Goliath, Saul is also exceptional and Goliath's natural opponent, based on his physical stature and his stature as king (1 Sam. 9:2). Yet he and all Israel are paralyzed by inaction and fear (1 Sam. 17:11).

David's Arrival at the Battlefield 1 SAMUEL 17:12–19

Jesse of Bethlehem sends his three oldest sons to bolster the Israelite army in their stand against the Philistines. Jesse asks his youngest son, the shepherd boy David, to bring supplies to his brothers and check on their welfare.

David's father, Jesse, is an Ephrathite (1 Sam. 17:12; the family of Naomi were also Ephrathites; Ruth 1:2). Ephrathah is either another name for Bethlehem or a region nearby, and it likely also identifies the name of a clan that settled there. At this early point in their history, Israel does not have a standing army. The people who gather to fight the Philistines are either those most loyal to the king (1 Sam. 14:52; 22:2) or the ones most affected by the outcome of the battle (e.g., Judg. 5:12–18). As the only significant Israelite town between the Philistine camp and Saul's home in Gibeah, the likely Philistine objective, Bethlehem stands to be overrun should Goliath win. Of course Jesse would have told his oldest sons, "Go help hold the line!"

Because Saul doesn't have a standing army, his force must rely in part on its own resourcefulness for basic needs. At Jesse's direction, David, the youngest son, brings his brothers food. The items consist of fare typical for the Judean hill country economy (mixed grain and goat-dairy), with the best going to the commander of their unit (i.e., "of their thousand;" 1 Sam. 17:17–18). The "ten cheeses" for the commander are likely made from curdled goat milk fortified with salt, then dried to a hard consistency so as to withstand the hot climate for months, sans refrigeration (it is still made today). The custom of bringing gifts to important people, always with the intent of currying favor down the road, is an age-old tradition still practiced in the Middle East. In this case, Jesse surely wants to encourage Saul to treat his boys well.

At this point in the story, we see something quite genuine about the heart of David. He does not go to Saul's camp with the idea of participating in the battle (let alone becoming the hero), nor does he want to shirk his home responsibilities for the sake of adventure. Rather, David makes the trip at the request of his father to check on his brothers' welfare, as a good brother should.

The Shepherd Boy's Decision 1 SAMUEL 17:20–40

Ignoring the scorn of his older brothers and the warnings of his king, David accepts the challenge to fight the giant. He chooses to meet Goliath alone and without armor, protected only by his sling and confidence in God.

An underlying motif in the story of David and Goliath is the value of honor versus the scorn of shame. The need to expunge shame and restore honor is a strong motivating factor in tribal society generally, and it has certainly played a role in personal and communal actions throughout the ancient Near East.

- Goliath tries to shame Israel by defying Saul, the Israelite army, and the Lord (1 Sam. 17:10, 25, 45).
- Saul brings shame on Israel by his fearful, indecisive lack of action when protocol demands that it is he who should be fighting Goliath (1 Sam. 17:11, 16).

- David's older brothers try to shame him by accusing him of selfish motives in coming down to the camp (1 Sam. 17:28).
- Saul speaks to the young David condescendingly, disdaining David's abilities because of his youth (1 Sam. 17:33).

With Israel's honor at stake (not to mention the practical matter of impending defeat on the battlefield), David is at first incredulous that no one is willing to erase the Philistine defilement of Israel, then firm in his ability to do so himself (1 Sam. 17:34–37). When David informs Saul of his skills in protecting his family's flocks, we see something of his character: he possesses the tough edge needed to protect living beings under his charge.

It was often the responsibility of the youngest son (or sometimes daughter) to tend the family flocks. That David is a shepherd does not denigrate him or needlessly heighten the contrast between him and either Saul or Goliath. Shepherding in the ancient Near East involved a set of tasks that honed skills of resourcefulness, persistence, and courage. Depending on the weather and location of available grass, the shepherd could be away from the provision and protection of his family home for days or weeks at a time. For this reason, he (or she) had to learn to live off the land like the flock under his care while defending his charges from all manner of danger, including wild animals looking for a fast-food meal. The only recourse was to develop one's own skill set—and depend on God.

Saul promises that the person who kills Goliath will receive great wealth, the king's daughter in marriage, and exemption from tax for his father's family (1 Sam. 17:25). Even though it is still quite early in the history of Israel's monarchy, we see that Saul has adopted the full-blown trappings of kingship. Most likely he feels that he can be generous because he has already taken in ways that Samuel warned that kings tend to do (1 Sam. 8:10–18). In any case, as we'll see, the story will end without any rewards given.

David's lack of armor and his simple, natural weapon (a sling and five river stones) contrasts sharply with Goliath's powerful armament. Manufactured slingstones—chipped spheres of limestone about the size of a tennis ball—have been found in archaeological excavations. David apparently doesn't have recourse to these, so instead he chooses five stones from the nearby stream that flows seasonally at the bottom of the Valley of Elah. (The stones he would grab as a shepherd to fight off lions and bears would be whatever was lying on the ground at the moment.) Scholars wonder why David chooses five stones rather than just one. Some suggest that he isn't sure that one will do the job and wants to be prepared for multiple shots. Others, based on battle notices recorded in 2 Samuel 21:15–22, posit that Goliath has four brothers, prompting David to gather enough stones to take all of them out should they try to take revenge after seeing Goliath fall.

David used simple river-washed stones, rather than formally manufactured slingshot stones.

In a nod to the invisible characters in Bible stories, we read of a shepherd whom David leaves to watch over the flock in his absence (1 Sam. 17:20), a keeper of baggage with Saul's army (1 Sam. 17:22), and Goliath's shield bearer (1 Sam. 17:7, 41)—all anonymous. These are three of hundreds of people whom we meet on the pages of Scripture who forever will be known only to God. Although the spotlight falls on Goliath, Saul, and David, the presence of these unnamed others is not incidental, for without them the main characters could not perform their roles. Using honorable language, David calls himself Saul's servant (1 Sam. 17:34); the real servants are the unsung workers whose service allows the story to happen.

The Beginning of the Battle 1 SAMUEL 17:41–51

After hearing Goliath's taunt, David drops the Philistine with a single stone from his sling, then kills him with the Philistine's own sword.

The battle action in the narrative begins with a physical description of David, one that matches what Samuel had seen when he first anointed David the future king (1 Sam. 16:12; 17:42). David is *admoni*, "ruddy," a term otherwise used only for the reddish newborn Esau (Gen. 25:25). Ruddy likely refers to David's natural complexion. As shepherds, both David and Esau spent much time out of doors and their natural looks no doubt were freshened by the elements. Some interpreters suggest that David is also a redhead, but red hair was extremely rare among Israelites of the time (not enough Indo-European DNA had entered the Israelite gene pool yet). David's ruddiness is tempered by the description "handsome." This word carries connotations of a person having a fair, beautiful appearance and is used in the Bible for both males and females. What Samuel no doubt saw as unstained potential, the metal-clad giant sees as a soft, pretty boy armed only with sticks.

Taunts intended to dehumanize the enemy have always been part of face-to-face combat (1 Sam. 17:36, 43–44). Spewing defilement, Goliath invokes his own gods when he curses David. This would have involved calling on their (presumed) power to bring disaster on the shepherd boy. By invoking the gods of the Philistines and assuming their role in victory, Goliath also declares their superiority over the Lord, the God of Israel. This, David cannot allow. Goliath boasts that he will give David "to the beasts of the field" (1 Sam. 17:44) while David replies that he will give the carcasses of the Philistine army "to the wild beasts of the earth" (1 Sam. 17:46). In both cases the taunt is one that denies the enemy a proper burial, a horrifying fate in a world structured around ancestral ties to family and land. But there may be more. The "wild beasts of the earth" of David's taunt are carnivorous animals, the kind that lurk on the edges of battlefields and scavenge for food. But "beasts of the field" are those found in grazing places: sheep, goats, donkeys, and cattle. Are the two phrases synonymous, their difference only a sign of literary creativity? Is Goliath's "beasts of the field" just a slip of the tongue since his native language is not Hebrew? Is Goliath saying that David is so weak that even the flocks that he herds will gobble him up? Or, as some commentators hold, is this more evidence that Goliath is coarse, unintelligent, and so overcome by blind impulse that he just blurts out nonsense?[7] That would make him easier prey for David.

A well-aimed slingstone—the resourceful weapon of a shepherd—hitting the head of Goliath knocks the giant over and he dies from the blow. The final stroke is decapitation, by Goliath's own sword no less. The Philistines may well have thought that their champion had only been stunned by the slingstone, but they now clearly see that he is dead, and panic *en masse*. The summary statement emphasizes David's victory despite the disparity of weapons: "So David prevailed over the Philistine with a sling and with a stone, and struck the Philistine and killed him. There was no sword in the hand of David" (1 Sam. 17:50).

The End of the Battle 1 SAMUEL 17:52–58

The men of Judah pursue the retreating Philistines deep into Philistine territory. Saul's response is to want to know more about David.

The account of the battle ends as it begins, with a geographical map of the action. Here we read the lines of retreat (1 Sam. 17:52). The Philistines flee back to their home cities, Gath at the western end of the Valley of Elah and Ekron at the western end of the Valley of Sorek just to its the north. The Valley of Sorek was the location of Samson's exploits against the Philistines a generation or so before (Judg. 13–16). This pushes the Philistines back to the coastal plain, completely out of Israelite territory. On the way, the battled passes by Shaaraim, which some scholars identify with Khirbet Qeiyafa, an archaeological site between Socoh and Azekah (1 Sam. 17:1). Excavations have found that Khirbet Qeiyafa appears to have been fortified specifically at the time of this battle.

With the rights of a victor, David takes Goliath's armor, but rather than turn it over to his superior, King Saul, he puts it in his own tent, perhaps all the way back at his home in Bethlehem (1 Sam. 17:54). Later (when, we do not know), Goliath's sword ends up in the custody of Ahimelech, the priest at Nob, an Israelite religious center on the Mount of Olives overlooking Jerusalem (1 Sam. 21:1, 9). The sanctuary at Nob seems to have gained prominence after the Philistines destroyed Shiloh and killed off Eli's priestly line (1 Sam. 4:1–11; Jer. 7:12). There Goliath's sword is carefully wrapped and kept as a relic of divine victory behind the ephod, the instrument by which the priests ascertain the will of God (Ex. 28:6–14; 1 Sam. 23:9–11; 30:7–8). When David flees from Saul some weeks or months after defeating Goliath, he takes the sword from Nob to use in future battles (1 Sam. 21:9; 22:9–10).

In the meantime, David takes Goliath's severed head to Jerusalem (1 Sam. 17:54). Here we see him acting as a true champion would in the ancient world. Severed heads are more portable than entire bodies and were often paraded around to friend and foe alike after a battle as the surest sign that an enemy was dead. The practice was meant to instill terror in the adversary and confidence in the victor. The ancient Egyptians sometimes piled up severed hands or even male genitalia for similar reasons, as David did later with Philistine foreskins (1 Sam. 18:24–27). But it is odd that David takes Goliath's head to Jerusalem since Jerusalem is still a Jebusite city, not yet under Israelite control. Speculation by commentators abounds, all the way from saying that "Jerusalem" was a code name for the Israelite

Khirbet Qeiyafa, which some scholars identify as Shaaraim, a place by which the retreating Philistines passed

sanctuary at Nob to the theologically convenient assertion that David must have buried Goliath's head at Golgotha, "Place of a Skull" (Matt. 27:33; Mark 15:22; John 19:17). In any case, the mention of Jerusalem does anticipate that the city will become Israelite under the later military action of King David (2 Sam. 5:6–10).

David With The Head Of Goliath (Alessandro Turchi, c. 1620)

The story of David and Goliath ends with a short conversation between Saul and his general, Abner, that seems to indicate that Saul doesn't know who David is (1 Sam. 17:55–58). The conversation seems out of place since the prior chapter relates how, in an intimate in-home scene, David has already served as Saul's music therapist, calming his dark moods. There David shows no pretense to the throne nor tips his hand that he possesses skills that could usurp the king, even though he has already been anointed by Samuel as Saul's successor. Perhaps we shouldn't read Saul's question to Abner ("Whose son is this youth?") as an inquiry of identity but one of incredulity ("*Who is this?!*"), with the same tone that Jesus's disciples wonder about their master after he had calmed the storm: "Who then is this, that even the wind and sea obey him?" (Mark 4:41). Saul likely also assumes that David's father must be an even greater warrior than the son. David's reply continues the protocol of obeisance: "I am the son of your servant Jesse the Bethlehemite" (1 Sam. 17:58). With it, we sense a foreshadowing of what will become David's greatest victory: his establishing from Bethlehem "the house and lineage of David" (Luke 2:4).

DAVID AND GOLIATH IN LATER WRITINGS

As significant as it was at the time, the battle of David versus Goliath is not mentioned again in the Hebrew Bible (Old Testament) or the New Testament. However, the Septuagint includes an additional psalm, Psalm 151, which is a poetic account of the early highlights of David's life. The psalm concludes with these lines:

> *I went out to meet the Philistine,*
> *And he cursed me by his idols.*
> *But I drew his own sword;*
> *I beheaded him,*
> *And removed reproach from the people of Israel.*

The life of David and the royal line that he founds become a unifying force throughout the Bible and Intertestamental literature, culminating in Jesus the Christ, the Messiah. In it we see the unfolding of the first two episodes of David's life: He is the great psalmist bringing comfort to a troubled world (1 Sam. 16:14–23; 2 Sam. 23:1; Amos 6:5; Ben Sirach (Ecclesiasticus) 47:8–10; Rom. 4:6–8; Heb 4:7), and he is the great warrior saving Israel from extinction (1 Sam. 17:1–58; 2 Sam. 8:1–14). In both roles, David exhibits skill, dexterity, promise, and courage—on the one hand comforting others while on the other acknowledging the help that God gives in battle. Both are necessary to reign as king, and both define the messianic hope that a Son of David will bring final victory over God's greatest enemy (Matt. 20:30–31; 21:9–15; Acts 1:6; 15:16–17).

Throughout the centuries, church fathers and Christian theologians have portrayed David as one of the most important Old Testament types, or pictures, of Christ. In contrast, they allegorize Goliath into Satan, the one who fights against Christ. An early Jewish tradition holds that Orpah was the sister of Ruth, and that after she returned to her Moabite home, she married Goliath, making David and Goliath kin by marriage! While this tradition surely is fanciful, it does recognize how up close and personal the struggle between good and evil, God and Satan, is in everyone.

Study Questions

1. What crises, as described in the book of 1 Samuel, does Israel face leading up to the story of David and Goliath?
2. How is King Saul portrayed in the story of David and Goliath? What could he have done differently to show himself to be an effective leader?
3. David declared, "The battle is the LORD's" (1 Sam. 17:47). Warfare, for better or worse, is a part of human history, and also of our world now. Do you think warfare language is still an appropriate way of describing the actions of God on behalf of his people today? Why or why not?
4. How is David portrayed in the story? Do you think his actions are above reproach throughout? Why or why not?
5. How does the story of David and Goliath prepare us to better understand why David was the founder of the messianic line?
6. The story of David versus Goliath is much more than a "little guy triumphs overs big guy" story. What are some of the larger lessons that we can learn?

Chapter 5 Notes

1 Josephus, *Antiquities of the Jews*, vi.156.
2 For a summary of Philistine battle tactics, armor, and their incursions toward Israel, see Boyd Seevers, *Warfare in the Old Testament: The Organization, Weapons, and Tactics of Ancient Near Eastern Armies* (Kregel, 2013), 145–81.
3 For these Bible stories, see Gen. 37:3–4, 19–20; Ex. 2:14; 4:10; Judg. 4:8; 6:11–15; 11:1–7; 1 Sam. 1:1–2, 10–11; 2:4–8; 17:12–15; Jer. 1:6; Amos 7:14–15; Est. 2:7; 4:14; Luke 1:26–29, 46–55; 2:46–47.
4 This is the logical suggestion of James M. Monson, *The Land Between: A Regional Study Guide to the Land of the Bible* (Biblical Backgrounds, 1983), 201–203.
5 4QSama; Josephus, *Antiquities of the Jews*, vi.171.
6 In particular, the reliefs on the walls of the Medinet Habu mortuary temple of Rameses III (12th century BC).
7 Maurice Samuel, *Certain People of the Book* (Union of American Hebrew Congregations, 1955), 99.

Chapter 5 Images

David with the Head of Goliath by Antonio del Castillo y Saavedra, 1616–1668, Yale University Art Gallery
Philistine Migration; satellite map courtesy of NASA
Philistine jug, The Israel Museum, Jerusalem
The Anointing of David by Samuel by Felix-Joseph Barrias, 1842
Elah Valley (Paul H. Wright)
The Battle of David and Goliath; satellite map courtesy of NASA
Philistine captives, Medinet Habu, the mortuary temple of Pharaoh Rameses III (Paul H. Wright)
River stones (Paul H. Wright)
Khirbet Qeiyafa (Abraham Greitzer/Wikimedia)
David with the Head of Goliath by Alessandro Turchi, c. 1620

Chapter 6

THE STORY OF JONAH

Jonah 1–4

IT'S A WHALE of a tale, this story of Jonah. We see Jonah running from God and then swallowed alive, only to live, dissent, and run another day. Some call Jonah the reluctant prophet. That's diplomatic. Petulant and grudging are perhaps more on the mark, at least if actions betray his words. His is a short tale, told in 48 verses, fewer than 700 words in Hebrew. These are divided into four distinct scenes, each relating an encounter involving our hero (or is he an anti-hero?) in ways perhaps too close to us for comfort. Jonah's name means "dove" or, in its more banal conception, "pigeon," a rather flighty bird (all associations of purity and peace aside). To the prophet Hosea, doves are "silly and without sense," like wayward Israel (Hos. 7:11). Jonah is well named.

The story of Jonah is full of suspense, intrigue, heroic behavior, and behavior something quite other. Throughout, it is told imaginatively, not in the sense of coming out of someone's vivid imagination but rather because it is evocative. Readers engage the action of Jonah's story by active visual participation, relayed with language that is plain yet sensational. Everything draws us in: blurred motives, characters acting out of character, questions asked that go unanswered, and things not possible that actually happen. This is indeed a whale of a story—whatever creature it is that swallows Jonah.

Jonah's is the only book of the English Bible that is counted as one of the books of the Prophets yet composed as narrative. In it, Jonah doesn't speak very often, and only five of his words (eight in English) are prophet-like: "Yet forty days, and Nineveh shall be overthrown!" (Jonah 3:4). We would like him to say a bit more, but to the reader his actions speak louder than his words. While the story seems to be pointed at Israel's Ninevite enemies, the object of its lesson is the prophet himself, a man who falls well short of the prophetic ideal. In fact, he isn't even called a prophet in his own story.

Scholars are fond of debating whether the story of Jonah is

- history—a description of an actual event;
- a parable—a very short story that, while not technically factual, is realistic enough for readers to draw analogies to their own lives;
- an extended allegory—a story, which may or may not have actually happened, that contains spiritual lessons expressed as types of behavior; or
- a midrash—a fanciful tale that seeks answers to religious questions.

While some of the happenings in the story are anything but normal, Nineveh and Joppa are real places, and Jonah's overall attitude is typical of what we might expect given what Israel is facing at the time. The usual reasons given for the story's non-historical nature are not these but rather have to do with the fish, the size of Nineveh, the unlikelihood that the city would repent, and the quick growth of the plant as Jonah waits God out. Yet these objections can be countered by a careful look at the data. If the story is fiction, its personal impact on readers is perhaps less intrusive, or at least not as permanent, as we might expect it to be if the events actually happened. Jesus, however, seems to recognize that the events are historical; his own statements about Jonah would lose some of their punch if they were compared to a fictional tale rather than reality itself (Matt. 12:39–41; 16:4; Luke 11:29–32).

It is probably best to characterize the book of Jonah as a prophetic teaching narrative, more similar to the books of Joshua, Judges, 1 and 2 Samuel, and 1 and 2 Kings (what the Hebrew Bible calls the Former

Prophets) than to the books of Isaiah through Malachi (the Latter Prophets). The books of Joshua through 2 Kings record historical events through the eyes of writers whose convictions are in line with those of the prophets. The difference, of course, is that rather than calling out the actions of Israel's leaders as the biblical prophets so readily do, the author of the book of Jonah (who was not likely Jonah) criticizes the prophet himself. The book is pointedly self-critical, and that fact, in and of itself, says something important about the maturity and reliability of the authors of the Bible.

Jonah the man is identified simply as "the son of Amittai" (Jonah 1:1). No other personal identification is given, not even that he is a prophet, and this lack of specific identity may prompt us to interpret the story free of a specific historic context. But astute Bible readers perhaps recall a "Jonah the son of Amittai" from 2 Kings 14:25, "the prophet, who was from Gath-hepher" whose word from the Lord that Israel would restore its borders "from Lebo-hamath as far as the Sea of the Arabah" is fulfilled in Jonah's own day.

Jonah lived during or a bit before the reign of Jeroboam II, who was king of the northern kingdom of Israel from 793 to 753 BC. This was a heady time. In the century before, an expanding Assyrian Empire, Israel's

The reconstructed Adad Gate on the northern end of ancient Nineveh. It was largely destroyed by ISIS forces in 2016.

most-feared enemy, had already reached Damascus and Mount Carmel. But now, as Assyrian strength ebbed somewhat, Jeroboam II pushed the borders of his kingdom far to the north, halfway to the Euphrates River. It was a brief moment of glory, with a booming economy, an effective military, heads held high, and a competent (though self-serving) royal administration. The book of Jonah fits well with this historical context in mind: a religious nationalist prophet happy to be part of the effort to keep his kingdom robust and personally opposed to anything that would strengthen Nineveh, the most significant city in Assyria, lest they rise again. But indeed they did.

Jonah's Gath-hepher was a lovely place to call home, situated just above a large, fertile valley, supplied by a strong spring and blessed by plenty of sunshine, ample rainfall, pleasant Mediterranean breezes—and square in the path of the Assyrian attack that was sure to come. Within half a century a resurgent Assyria will conquer Galilee, including the ridge on which Jonah's hometown stands, then destroy his Israelite kingdom (2 Kings 15:29; 17:5–6). In historical hindsight, Jonah's own descendants paid the ultimate tangible price because Nineveh was not destroyed at his prophetic word. But all this context isn't mentioned in the book that bears Jonah's name. *His* tale is much more about a conversation between himself and the Lord, and how great God's compassion for others actually is. Personal cost, unmentioned, is understood.

Themes in the Story of Jonah

God's compassion is universal.

It was common for people in the ancient world to believe in national deities. These were territorial gods, each fighting on behalf of a particular king and his subjects (1 Kings 20:23; 2 Kings 18:33–35). Mirroring the desires of their regent kings, national gods sought to expand their control in heaven and on earth through conquest, crossing boundaries into the territories of other national gods in the process. What these deities didn't do was care for foreigners (indeed, they scarcely cared about their own

The Journeys of Jonah

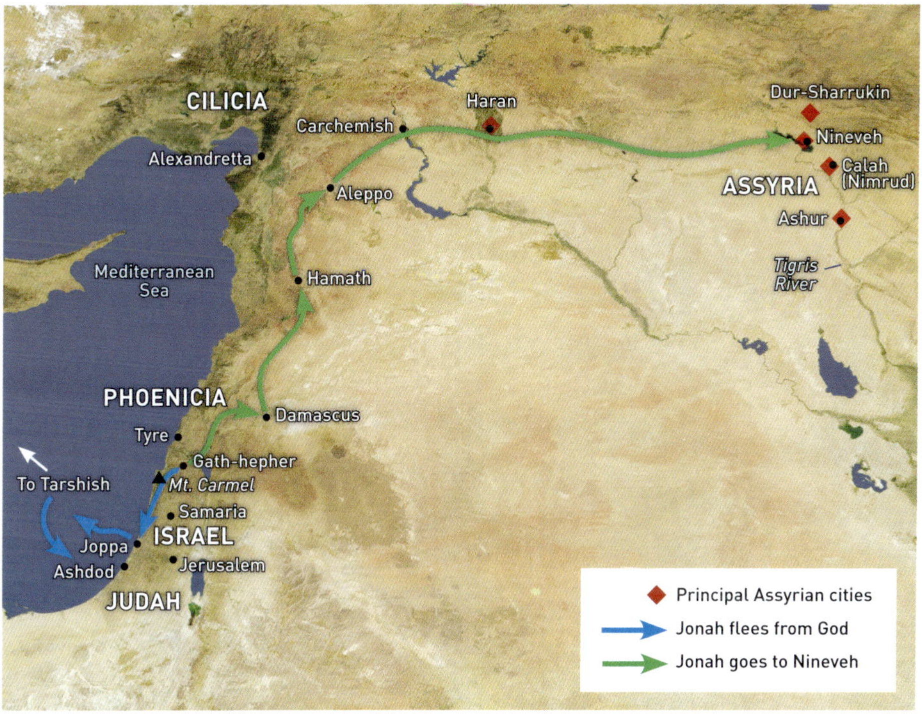

people). Jonah, also not caring about others, tries to flee from the Lord by going down to Joppa and then out on the open sea, only to find out that the Lord is already there, not to mention present in a place as hostile as Nineveh (cf. Ps. 139:7–12).

More importantly, Jonah finds that God is also compassionate to people outside Israel's borders. The Bible is clear that God reserves the right to respond positively to people who repent, even those who might not otherwise seem, from our vantage point, to be able or deserve to do so (1 Kings 21:27–29; 2 Kings 20:1–6; Jer. 18:1–11; Rom. 9:15). In his head, Jonah knows that God is "gracious … and merciful, slow to anger and abounding in steadfast love, and relenting from disaster," a declaration often repeated in the Bible (Jonah 4:2). God is free; he is not able to be controlled. He stands above our expectations, wishes, and power structures. Yet Jonah wants to stuff God's compassion into a box, limit it, let only some of it out. It is God's active compassion for a place as lost as Nineveh that shows us what his character really is. By comparison, this also says a lot about Jonah. God's message of good news, stubbornly resisted by the prophet, flows from Isaiah (who also faced the Assyrian threat; Isa. 2:2–4; 19:21; 60:1–9) into the Gospels (Luke 4:24–27; John 3:16) and then to us.

God wants everyone to repent.

God is not only compassionate but desires that everyone find him (John 10:9; Acts 2:21; Rom. 10:12–13; 1 Tim. 2:4). While divine justice is real, God is willing to relent—that is, to allow his commands for judgment to be conditional upon repentance (Ex. 32:11–14; 2 Chron. 7:14; Jer. 18:7–8; 26:3; Jonah 3:9). Everyone has the capacity to consciously and willingly repent, allowing God to fill up the divine image that he has placed in us according to his character.

Knowing about God is not the same thing as knowing God.

Jonah is the poster child of the truth that knowing facts *about* God is very different from knowing him. Jonah knows that God—the Lord—is the creator of the universe (Jonah 1:9). He knows how to pray, make vows, and offer sacrifices in the temple (Jonah 2:7–9). He even knows that God is compassionate (Jonah 4:2). But it is the sinner, not the one who appears righteous, who most acutely recognizes the need to be forgiven—and to forgive. The love of Christ, we read in Ephesians 3:18–19, surpasses knowledge, and the actions that are acceptable to God, unlike those of Jonah, are those that flow from a contrite heart (Isa. 1:11–17; Mic. 6:8; Luke 18:9–14).

Miracles happen.

When we add up the number of chapters in the Bible that are narrative, we see that most of the time God is either acting within the flow of normal human events or is standing behind the scenes. Only a relatively few chapters contain stories in which God breaks into history and alters the laws of nature. These cluster around the lives of Moses, Elijah, Daniel, Jesus, and the early apostles; and all happen at critical moments in Israel's history. When reading or hearing a miracle story, like Jonah's, skeptics (and a good many realists) dismiss it with, "It just *can't* happen." But when we change the word order to "It can't *just* happen," we put the emphasis back where it needs to be. Miracles don't *just* happen without God stepping in. By definition, a God who creates and who is free can also intervene in his creation any way he sees fit. Take God out of the formulas that determine the laws of nature and things only happen the way we expect them to. Put God back in and everything becomes possible—or, in the words of Jesus, "With man this is impossible, but with God all things are possible" (Matt. 19:26; cf. Gen. 18:14; Job 42:2; Jer. 32:17; Zech. 8:6; Luke 1:37).

Events in the Story of Jonah

Scene 1: Jonah's Encounter with the Pagan Mariners JONAH 1:1–17

Called by the Lord to speak God's judgment on Nineveh, Jonah instead runs the other way and boards a ship for Tarshish. After the Lord causes a violent storm that threatens the ship, Jonah tells the mariners to throw him overboard to calm the sea. They do, and he is swallowed by a great fish.

Only two characters are given personal names in Jonah's story: he and the Lord. All others—the mariners, the Ninevites, the king of Nineveh, and, yes, the fish and the plant—are unnamed. Because of this, the storyteller leads us to read the plotline as a conversation between Jonah and the Lord. All the other action happens for the sole purpose of revealing their true natures. Jonah, "dove," is flighty and unpredictable. The Lord, whose name *Yahweh* comes from the Hebrew verb for "to be," is wholly concerned about life.

Called to "arise" (as prophets are supposed to do; Jonah 1:2; cf. Josh. 1:2; 1 Sam. 16:12; 1 Kings 17:9; 21:17–18; Jer. 1:17; Ezek. 3:22; Acts 8:26),

Jonah instead goes down to Joppa, down to a ship, down to the hold of the ship, and eventually down to the bottom of the sea (Jonah 1:3, 5; 2:5–6). The verbs *arise* and *go down*, which are part of the narrative in Hebrew, are often translated by other phrases in English versions of the Bible, such as "went aboard" or "had gone below deck." But what makes for good English style sometimes obscures the force of the action. Biblical Hebrew uses repetition of words for emphasis, while good English style favors a liberal use of synonyms. By noticing repetitions in the story of Jonah, we are better able to sense the passion, even the melodrama, of the action. The intensity of the drama is signaled by the Hebrew adjective *gadol*, "great" or "important," which appears fourteen times in the book. The wind (Jonah 1:4), the storm (1:4, 12), the mariner's terror (1:10), their fear (1:16), and the fish (1:17) are all *gadol*. So are Nineveh (1:2; 3:2, 3; 4:11), its inhabitants (3:5) and nobles ("great ones," 3:7), and Jonah's displeasure (4:1) and his joy (as temporary as that was; 4:6). Interspersed is the contrasting adjective *ra'*, "bad" or "evil," describing the calamitous trouble brought on by the storm (1:7–8), the character of the Ninevites (1:2; 3:8, 10), the disaster threatened by God (3:10), and the displeasure and discomfort of Jonah at it all (4:1, 6). In another repetition of words, the Lord "appointed" the fish to swallow Jonah (1:17), the plant to shade Jonah (4:6), the worm to kill the plant (4:7), and the wind to torture him (4:8).

The breakwater and harbor of modern Jaffa (ancient Joppa) south of Tel Aviv

Important details about the initial conversation between the Lord and Jonah elude us. We are not told what God tells him to say to the Ninevites, nor does Jonah reply with words. As the story unfolds, we are left to ponder his motive for going "down … away from the presence of the Lord" (Jonah 1:3). Does Jonah think himself unworthy to deliver a prophetic message, as did Moses, Isaiah, and Jeremiah (Ex. 3:11; 4:1, 10, 13; Isa. 6:4–7; Jer. 1:4–10)? Is he a coward? Assyria certainly had a reputation for cruelty to foreigners (Nahum 3:1, 10, 19). Does Jonah not want to come to terms with the ramifications of a God who is compassionate to everyone, when "everyone" includes his mortal enemy? Or is this just a visceral reaction, something explained by panic in his gut? And in running, does Jonah think that God's presence is localized to Israel? Does he hope to actually flee? And how can he fall asleep at a time like this (Jonah 1:5–6)?

Jonah not only goes down but runs in the opposite direction from Nineveh. There are seaports a day's walk from Jonah's Gath-hepher home, but he instead flees south to Joppa to head out to open sea toward Tarshish. While the location of Tarshish is unknown (suggestions include Cilicia, North Africa, Italy, and Spain), the name carries connotations of an exotic place about as far away as a boat can go. Joppa and Tarshish were connected by sea routes linking the Mediterranean world, which at the time was dominated by the Phoenicians, Israel's commercial neighbor to the north. Although not specified as such, the mariners in the Jonah story are most likely Phoenicians, whose maritime skills are described in detail in Ezekiel 27.

As a whole, ancient Israelites feared the sea, viewing it with the kind of healthy respect that accompanies something altogether beyond one's control. Canaanite mythology (to which the Phoenician mariners ascribed) conceived that the god of the sea, Yamm, was the personification of sudden, uncontrolled chaos and death. To counter this idea, the Bible frequently portrays God's lordship as victory over the sea: "You rule the raging of the sea; when its waves rise, you still them" (Ps. 89:9; cf. Pss. 33:7; 65:7; 107:29; Isa. 27:1; 51:10; Matt. 8:23–27; 14:22–33). This is seen with creation, as God pushes the deep waters aside so that people will have a place to live (Gen. 1:9–10), and in the new heavens and new earth where there is no longer any sea

Phoenician ship, depicted on a sarcophagus (2nd century AD)

(Rev. 21:1). Though Jonah is a landlubber from the hilly center of Galilee, he certainly knows the sea's volatile reputation and so identifies himself to the mariners as a devotee of the Lord God "who made the sea" (Jonah 1:9). Clearly the storm that nearly sinks Jonah's ship is an act of God (Jonah 1:4), something wholly unexpected since ships normally don't sail during the stormy season. But as Creator, God also holds the power to calm the sea in an instant.

The mariners, who are polytheists, don't know which god is responsible for the storm that threatens their ship and the lives of everyone on board. Each prays to his own god and asks the passengers to do the same. By casting lots, the mariners correctly select Jonah as the responsible party. In the Bible and the ancient Near East generally, lots were cast to determine the will of God or the gods, to divide property or spoil, or to organize rotations in temple service (Josh. 18:6; Neh. 11:1; Est. 3:7; Joel 3:3; Obad. 11; Nah. 3:10; Acts 1:26). Sometimes the lots resembled dice. Here, casting lots confirms the sovereignty of God, not only in his ability to control the powers of nature, but also the decisions and actions of the pagan mariners (cf. Prov. 16:33).

Dice typical of the ancient Mediterranean world

The genuine concern shown to Jonah by the mariners contrasts greatly with Jonah's complete insensitivity to the moment. By nature, mariners live in constant contact with foreigners, including strangers with all sorts of rough edges. But at sea on a vessel that is in effect an island unto itself, the mariners temper their own coarseness to care for those under their charge. To do so at all costs is the code of the sea. It is the mariners, not Jonah, who bring up the subject of God and prayer. Even when the mariners know that their own distress—and likely demise—is due to Jonah's actions, they choose, as the scene builds to a terrifying crescendo, to do everything they can to save this guilty stranger in their midst (Jonah 1:5–13). Pagans all, the mariners even come to recognize that the sovereignty of the Lord is greater than human will (Jonah 1:14). Sleepy Jonah, in contrast, asks the mariners to break their code of honor by throwing him into the sea. Is Jonah suicidal? Is this a last-minute confession stemming from acknowledgment of guilt? Is Jonah ashamed now that his prior actions have been found out? Is he hoping that self-sacrifice will appease God and save the mariners? Perhaps we should give credit to Jonah in thinking that he seems to know that a moral God won't punish the innocent (an innocent Israelite at least), and so he wants to be handed over to him, whatever the consequences of his personal actions may be. Jonah has no reason to expect that his life will be saved. For the pagan mariners, every single life is precious. For Jonah, not so much.

How are we to reconcile Jonah's confession in verse 9—"I am a Hebrew, and I fear the LORD"—with his actions in running away? Can we believe what he says, or do actions speak louder than words? Is he genuine, or parroting a nice theological position? In contrast to the sincerity and concern of the mariners, Jonah's words seem callous and rote, or at best reveal a man resigned to his fate. This scene anticipates similar actions and attitudes when Jonah encounters the people of Nineveh.

In spite of himself, and with no apparent intention to do so, Jonah's speech and actions convert the pagan mariners: "The men feared the LORD exceedingly, and they offered a sacrifice to the LORD and made vows" (Jonah 1:16). We don't know how and what they sacrifice (aboard ship might not be the best place for that) or the nature of their vows. But that the mariners do so "to the LORD" indicates a kind of conversion, even if it is only to acknowledge the particular power of one God among many (cf. Rom. 1:19–20).

The Lord appoints "a great fish" to swallow Jonah (Jonah 1:17). Scholars debate the identity and nature of the fish. Biblical Hebrew does not have a different word for whales, so it is lexically possible that the "great fish" (*dag gadol*) was actually a large aquatic mammal. Of all known whales, only the sperm whale has a throat wide enough to swallow something as large as a human. Occasional sailor stories speak of unfortunate mariners managing to stay alive in a sperm whale's laryngeal pouch due to air moving through, though becoming permanently disfigured from having bathed in the beast's gastric acid in the process. Yet an appeal to "something like the Jonah story actually has happened" is not particularly helpful in ferreting out the message of the book, since the episode of the fish (or whale) is only a portion of a much more significant plotline.

Sperm whale and calf

Still, Jonah's fish-bait-fate has all the markings of a miracle. Some interpreters believe that the fish was a special act of creation, something that totally contravened the normal laws of nature. Others suggest that what is miraculous is that the fish happened to be in the right place at the right time, an example of God working within nature as he did when he caused a strong east wind to separate the waters of the Red Sea at the exodus (Ex. 14:21). Either is possible; both are miraculous. It is significant that the narrator does not call the fish Leviathan, the sea monster of Canaanite myth in which the pagan mariners would have believed. Leviathan is occasionally mentioned in the Bible as a way of noting that God controls even the destructive things of this world (Pss. 74:13–14; 104:26). By not identifying the great fish as Leviathan, the Jonah story stands outside of what even Israel's neighbors considered normal.

Scene 2: Jonah's Encounter with God JONAH 2:1–10

Jonah prays to the Lord while inside the fish. The Lord commands the fish to disgorge Jonah onto dry land.

God does not appoint the great fish, whatever its genus and species, to punish Jonah but rather rescue him from certain death. For the reader, the fish is clear evidence of the truth of Jonah's confession that he knows God to be gracious, the one "relenting from disaster" (Jonah 4:2), whether Jonah understands what's going on or not.

Jonah speaks to God while in the belly of the fish. He uses poetry rather than everyday speech. In the ancient world, people typically used formal, refined, and weighty speech often spoken poetically when addressing a superior. Poetry allows a speaker to say things with more intensity than does common prose and to reveal his or her personal feelings with more expression than otherwise.

None of the lines in Jonah's prayer are original to him. Everything he says is found either verbatim or voiced with similar language in the Psalms:

JONAH	PSALMS
"I called out to the LORD, out of my distress, and he answered me" (2:2).	"I cried aloud to the LORD, and he answered me from his holy hill" (3:4; also 18:4–6; 118:5; 120:1; 130:1).
"For you cast me into the deep, into the heart of the seas" (2:3).	"You have put me in the depths of the pit, in the regions dark and deep" (88:6–7; also 42:7).
"I am driven away from your sight; yet I shall again look upon your holy temple" (2:4).	"I am cut off from your sight" (31:22). "I will bow down toward your holy temple" (5:7).
"The waters closed in over me to take my life; the deep surrounded me" (2:5).	"For the waters have come up to my neck. I sink in deep mire" (69:1–2).
"You brought up my life from the pit, O LORD my God" (2:6).	"O LORD, you have brought up my soul from Sheol; you restored me to life from among those who go down to the pit" (30:3; also 49:15; 56:13; 103:4).
"When my life was fainting away, I remembered the LORD, and my prayer came to you, into your holy temple. (2:7).	"When my spirit faints within me, you know my way! (142:3; also 107:5). "From his temple he heard my voice" (18:6).

JONAH	PSALMS
"Those who pay regard to vain idols forsake their hope of steadfast love" (2:8).	"I hate those who pay regard to worthless idols, but I trust in the LORD" (31:6).
"I with the voice of thanksgiving will sacrifice to you.... Salvation belongs to the LORD!" (2:9).	"Salvation belongs to the LORD" (3:8; also 37:39). "Offer to God a sacrifice of thanksgiving" (50:14; also 69:30; 107:22).

In times of trouble, or if asked to express our thoughts to God, our minds tend to go to words or ideas from familiar hymns or worship songs. So too Jonah, who knows the language of ancient Israel's hymnody. Jonah prays a psalm of a drowning man, describing someone sinking ever deeper into the waves and the seaweed, all the way down to the roots of the mountains where the bars of the grave close forever. In the first half of his prayer he is as good as dead, but by the end he knows that God has heard his cry and so responds to him with thanksgiving and a promise to sacrifice and make good on his vows. So far so good, if we can believe him. But given Jonah's prior attitude—not to mention his insolence once he arrives in Nineveh—his prayer seems a bit odd. There is no confession, no repentance, no penitence or regret, not even an acknowledgment of personal responsibility for his own actions. And Jonah blames God for hurling him into the sea rather than owning up to it himself (Jonah 2:3). He also discounts the faithful actions of the mariners who did all they could to save his life, those pagans "who pay regard to vain idols [and] forsake their hope of steadfast love" (Jonah 2:8). We are left with the impression that Jonah is speaking like someone who knows his Bible and expects to get out of trouble because he parrots the right things, rote or not. That Jonah is saved is due to the sovereignty of God, not Jonah's own endeavors or heart attitude.

"The LORD spoke to the fish, and it vomited Jonah out upon the dry land" (Jonah 2:10). The dry land onto which the fish vomits Jonah reminds us of the Bible's accounts of creation, the flood, and the exodus from Egypt. In each case, God provides dry land—a place suitable for human life—out of a watery abyss (Gen. 1:2, 9; 8:5–17; Ex. 14:21–22). There is much speculation, as well as local tradition, about the location of the dry land onto which Jonah is vomited. Suggestions both ancient and modern include Ashdod (just south of Joppa), Alexandretta (the Mediterranean port closest to Nineveh), somewhere along the Phoenician coast (where a fish-god was worshiped), or even the Black Sea.

Scene 3: Jonah's Encounter with the Pagan Ninevites JONAH 3:1–10

After the Lord calls Jonah a second time, he travels to Nineveh and warns everyone that their city will be destroyed. The people of Nineveh repent, and the Lord spares them from destruction.

Scene three opens with God once again telling Jonah to "Arise, go to Nineveh" (Jonah 3:2). We don't know how much time passes between Jonah's first and second callings. He must have needed some time to recover physically and emotionally, not to mention ponder what has happened to him and why. In any case, this time Jonah gets up and heads where he is intended to go.

Archaeological site of Nineveh in modern-day Mosul, Iraq

The ruins of ancient Nineveh, now extensively excavated, are near Mosul in northern Iraq. The city sat on the east bank of the Tigris River and was bisected by one of the river's tributaries. Nineveh's excavated remains reveal massive temples, palaces, and public gardens. Local tradition labels one of the mounds which housed an Assyrian palace or arsenal *Nebi Yunus*, "Prophet Jonah." Jonah 4:11 mentions that the population of Nineveh was more than 120,000 people, making it at least five times larger than the Jerusalem of Jonah's day. The city was surrounded by a flat plain, and its associated villages spread throughout the province, also called Nineveh. The wall that surrounded the city of Nineveh in the days of the Assyrian king Sennacherib, who made Nineveh the capital of Assyria a few decades after Jonah, measured eight miles (13 km) in circumference. Most scholars assume that the story's claim that Nineveh was "three days' journey in breadth" refers not to the walled city but its surrounding province (Jonah 3:3). Others suggest that it took Jonah three days to repeat his message up and down every street of town, or perhaps that his visit simply required three days. Yet the story of Jonah is clear that the greatness of Nineveh lay not in its size and grandeur but in its importance to God.

Assyrian King Sennacherib (705–681 BC)

We are not told what message God wants Jonah to proclaim in Nineveh, only what Jonah actually says: "Yet forty days, and Nineveh shall be overthrown!" (Jonah 3:4). In spite of what he has just personally experienced, Jonah frames his message around his conviction that God is a God of wrath, at least for Jonah's enemies. This is very different from Abraham's plea to God that Sodom and Gomorrah, equally wicked cities, be saved from destruction (Gen. 18:16–33).

Jonah's cry must have resonated with the Ninevites, for they and their king recognize they have offended God, call to him urgently, and "turn from [their] way and from the violence that is in [their] hands" (Jonah 3:7–8). But how might we understand the Ninevite response, given that we are not told that Jonah ever mentions God. Nor is there any indication that Jonah speaks of monotheism or the gracious character of the Lord or that he reveals any of the moral and ethical demands given by God through Moses. Jonah doesn't pitch a message of salvation, nor does he voice any hope that Nineveh might be spared.

The Ninevites probably knew that their country was in a period of national weakness. If so, we might suppose that they would have been sensitive to prophetic voices announcing their impending doom, though their reaction to a foreign voice from a far-off land is indeed perplexing. The Ninevites defined sin as improper behavior toward others, especially things done to offend their national deity, Ashur. From Assyrian texts we know that the Ninevites knew that their personal imperfections overwhelmed their capacity to do right and so lived in constant dread of punishment by the gods. Divine wrath, they believed, could be expiated through contrite actions, sacrifice, and invoking the gods for mercy.

Jonah Preaching to the Ninevites (Gustave Doré, 1866)

What we don't know is to which deity each of the Ninevites were praying so as to avert their impending destruction as a result of Jonah's pronouncement, since Jonah never mentions the name of the Lord his God. While the mariners, we read, "feared the Lord [Yahweh] exceedingly" (Jonah 1:16), the Ninevites "believed God [*Elohim*]" (Jonah 3:5). *Elohim* is the general Hebrew term for a deity. Depending on the context, the word *Elohim* can be rendered either "God" or "gods" in the Hebrew Bible. Here, English translations unanimously read "God," but because there was a temple to Ashur in Nineveh, we might wonder how many Ninevites turned their eyes there after Jonah's message.

In any case, like the mariners, Nineveh repents and holds out hope that God will be merciful (Jonah 3:5, 8–9). Is theirs a conversion to the God of the Bible or an indication that God honors repentance wherever he sees it? The story does not give a clear answer. How is it that the most important city in Assyria, with a huge population and its own established religious traditions, would immediately listen to an unknown man from a tiny village outside of their empire about a God they didn't know and who was wholly foreign to them? Indeed, this is a greater miracle than survival in a fish and a massive testimony to the sovereignty of God.

The Ninevites don sackcloth (Jonah 3:5–8). Sackcloth is coarse garb, probably woven from goat hair (the material of tents), worn by the poor, prisoners, slaves, and mourners (Ezek. 7:18; Joel 1:8, 13). By donning the scratchy clothing of mourners, the Ninevites may be wanting to show that they are slaves of God. There is no need to question their sincerity. The animals of Nineveh also fast and wear sackcloth. While this may be hyperbole on the part of the king's proclamation, it is consistent with the biblical worldview that all living things—whether they have immortal souls or not—are connected through a common creator. The Bible teaches that when people sin, the land and every living thing on it suffers and mourns (Deut. 28:15–68; Amos 1:2).

Sackcloth is woven from coarse goat hair.

Jonah's doomsday prediction in forty days comes and goes without a catastrophe. At the end of this scene, we read the reason: "When God saw what they did, how they turned from their evil way, God relented of the disaster that he had said he would do to them, and he did not do it" (Jonah 3:10).

Scene 4: Jonah's Encounter with God—Again JONAH 4:1–11

Jonah challenges the Lord, because God shows compassion on Nineveh. God's response is to prompt Jonah to want to admit that everyone is worthy of compassion. The story ends without Jonah's response.

This last scene opens with Jonah voicing a prayer that is a protest against God's character. Like his prayer in the belly of the fish, this one also quotes Scripture (Jonah 4:2; cf. Ex. 34:6–7; Neh. 9:17–18; Pss. 86:15; 103:8–14; 111:4; 112:4–5; 116:5–6; 145:8–12; Joel 2:13–14; James 5:11). Jonah's prayer reveals, at least in part, why he fled in the first place: he knows that God is compassionate, and Jonah apparently doesn't want that compassion to embrace Israel's mortal enemy. God is a God of overflowing compassion; Jonah is a prophet of wrath (or, as he might say, a prophet who places his own people first. And what's wrong—we might tend to ask—with that?). Nineveh, so he reasons, deserves the sharp edge of justice for what they stand to do to God's chosen people, Israel. This dissonance weighs heavily on the prophet, so much so that Jonah begs God to "take my life from me, for it is better for me to die than to live" (Jonah 4:3).

Why, for the second time in this short story, does Jonah want to die? A common suggestion in early Jewish (rabbinic) texts is that Jonah fears he will be labeled a false prophet, a stigma that will deprive him of honor, integrity, and meaning in life.[1] In a prior instance, Jonah's prophecy—that Israel expand its borders—was fulfilled (2 Kings 14:25). This time, Jonah's cry that Nineveh be destroyed is overruled by God. From the vantage point of everyone who witnessed the event, God simply does nothing. No angel of death passes over the city, no walls come crashing down, no one falls over in the street. A prophet who once was heralded at home simply can't return having been publicly refuted by his own God abroad. Other scholars suggest that Jonah is shamed because he knows that he is the instrument by which God spares Nineveh, only to have the Ninevites live to conquer Israel another day (which they did). In either case, Jonah's response is that of a bigot whose religious nationalistic feelings exclude care for anyone but his own people.

Jonah retreats from Nineveh to sit on a hill east of the city, awaiting its impending fate. There he poses as the poster child for petulance. What Jonah doesn't realize is that his own fate, not that of the Ninevites, is what is under divine inspection.

Just as God had appointed a great fish earlier (Jonah 1:17), here God appoints a plant to save miserable Jonah (Jonah 4:6). The plant is a *qiqayon*, a term that occurs only here in the Bible. Because it grows fast, most interpreters think it is a kind of ivy, or, following the Septuagint (third century BC), a gourd. The church father Jerome suggested that the *qiqayon* was a plant like the castor-oil plant (*Ricinus communis*), which grows quickly and stands upright without support.[2] In any case, the plant's quick growth may also be hyperbole. The result was a little shade, a huge relief from the intense Middle Eastern sun. Both the fish and the plant, and even the worm that withers the plant (also appointed by God), do what they were created to do; Jonah, on the other hand, does not.

Castor-oil plant

Next, Jonah is discomforted by "a scorching east wind" (Jonah 4:8). The modifier *scorching* comes either from a Hebrew verb that means "to be silent," hence sultry, or "to plow," hence cutting (the Hebrew words are homonyms). It seems to have been the hot, dry wind known as a sirocco, or *hamsin*, that saps life from all living things in the Middle East. The dry wind blowing from the east (the direction from which Jonah overlooks Nineveh) is a metaphor of God's judgment throughout the Bible (Ps. 48:7; Isa. 27:8; Jer. 4:11; 18:17; Ezek. 17:10; 19:12; Hos. 13:15).

God is concerned about Nineveh, "that great city" that held over 120,000 people, "and also much cattle," a term indicating all animal life (Jonah 4:11). The reference to people and animals indicates the wholeness of Ninevite life, in which people and animals are codependent and both deserve mercy from God. "These all look to you," says the psalmist, "to give them their food in due season" (Ps. 104:27). Indeed, the phrase "and also much cattle" is the last phrase in the Hebrew text of the story, punctuating the entire narrative with the full reach of God's compassion and care.

The story of Jonah does not end with a missionary call or any other call to action, other than to prompt us, the readers, to answer a rhetorical question from the Lord: "Should not I pity Nineveh, that great city, in which there are more than 120,000 persons who do not know their right hand from their left, and also much cattle?" (Jonah 4:11). Answering correctly is a prerequisite for whatever action God may call us to do. But by ending the story short of Jonah's reply, the answer may not be as obvious to everyone as it should be. Jonah is still running, not wanting to see or to change. His reticence prompts us to provide an answer for our own Ninevehs, whatever they may be. Perhaps the greatest miracle in the story is that God can save even Jonah—and even a Jonah today.

HEART QUESTIONS

In the narrative, God responds by asking questions, each more penetrating that the last, aimed squarely at Jonah's heart. Prompting conversations by asking questions rather than making pronouncements, as God does with Jonah, becomes a typically Jewish way of teaching. The Gospels, for instance, record that Jesus often stirs conversation by asking a question (e.g., Matt. 9:28; 12:3, 11, 48; 15:3, 16; 16:13, 15; 17:25; 19:17; 20:21; 21:28; John 5:6; 6:61; 10:32; 13:12; 18:34; 21:5, 15–17).

JONAH IN LATER WRITINGS

Because the story of Jonah hits so close to home, storytellers throughout the ages have found it to be fertile ground for harvesting motifs, motives, and memes for their own works of literature. From William Blake (*The Four Zoas*) to Daniel Defoe (*Robinson Crusoe*) to Herman Melville (*Moby Dick*) and Robert Frost (*A Masque of Mercy*)—writers have dipped into the story of Jonah to bolster their own characters, people who also strive to make sense out of forces much stronger than themselves. The process of emending the story actually began quite early, as interpreters from the time of the New Testament rewrote parts of it to justify their own understanding of God's sovereignty, given the world in which they lived:

- In *Antiquities of the Jews*, written at the end of the first century AD, the Jewish historian Josephus claimed to tell the story of Jonah "as I have found it written down," that is, as it is in the Bible.[3] Yet he stops his rendition with Jonah's cry to Nineveh (Jonah 3:4). Josephus says nothing about repentance or salvation, only that Nineveh would "lose their dominion in Asia." Josephus's Nineveh was Rome, and it seems that he wanted his Roman readers to think that the God of Israel bears no love for the people who destroyed the Jerusalem temple in his own day.
- The Dead Sea Scrolls, dating about a century earlier than Josephus, include ten scrolls of the Minor Prophets (Hosea through Malachi), but the book of Jonah is found in only five of them. The Dead Sea Scrolls that contain commentaries on the Bible also largely ignore Jonah. It seems that the message of God forgiving Nineveh was not very popular with the community who produced the scrolls, given that they, too, were threatened by Rome.
- The apocryphal book of 3 Maccabees, written in the first century BC, claims that after Jonah was vomited by the fish, God restored him, uninjured, and returned him to his family.[4] God did so, the writer says, to show that even though Israel was maligned among the nations, God would restore his people.
- Jewish midrash from the centuries following the New Testament tell us that the mariners represented the seventy people groups that comprised the heathen world, yet after the storm ceased, they

threw their idols in the sea, went up to Jerusalem, and became sages dedicated to the Lord.[5] It's a nice thought but one probably shaped by hopes that Judaism would triumph in spite of attacks by both paganism and Christianity.

In contrast, the Gospels don't change the storyline of the book of Jonah but do explain how Jonah points to Jesus:

- As Jonah was in the belly of the fish for three days (but for the grace of God, a place of certain death), so the Son of Man (this is Jesus's messianic title) will be in the heart of the earth for three days and three nights (Matt. 12:39–40). This speaks of Jesus's resurrection. Indeed, Jonah appears as a picture of the resurrection of Christ in many catacomb paintings in Rome.
- Jesus also contrasts the repentance of the Ninevites with the lack of repentance of people in his own generation: they will condemn you, Jesus said, "and behold, something greater than Jonah is here" (Matt. 12:41; cf. Luke 11:29–32). The ruins of Gath-hepher, Jonah's hometown, lay close to Nazareth, giving an extra punch to Jesus's words.

An early Christian catacomb fresco, depicting Jonah cast into the sea

The early church fathers saw the Jonah story as a picture of repentance and the universal extent of God's grace to the gentiles. They also portrayed Jonah as a type of Adam's fall and Jesus's descent to hell following the crucifixion prior to his resurrection.[6] The writers of the Protestant Reformation focused on Jonah's inner character, the struggle of everyone who is fallible yet saved by grace.[7]

Study Questions

1. The story of Jonah is told in a way that makes it pointedly self-critical. Why do you think the Bible includes a book that critiques God's own prophet?
2. What can we learn about God from his response to the actions of the mariners, the Ninevites, and the king of Nineveh? Who might be some modern equivalents of these characters?
3. Reflect on the words that Jonah prays in the fish's belly. How well do they mesh with his actions? Are they a window into his later behavior? How so?
4. What are some things that the author of the story of Jonah doesn't tell us that you wish he did? How does not knowing all of the details prompt us to interact with the story?
5. What is the greatest miracle in the story of Jonah? Why?
6. How would *you* answer God's final question to Jonah? How might this question be rephrased for today's context?

Chapter 6 Notes

1 *Midrash Jonah.*
2 Jerome, *Letter from Jerome to Augustine,* 7.22.
3 Josephus, *Antiquities of the Jews*, ix.205–214.
4 3 Maccabees 6:8–9.
5 *Midrash Jonah.*
6 St. Irenaeus, *Adversus haereses,* 3.20.1; Jerome, *In Jonam*, 422; St. Cyril of Jerusalem, *Catechetical Lectures*, 14.17–20.
7 John Calvin, *Commentary of the Prophet Jonah*; Martin Luther, *Lectures on Jonah*; William Tyndale, *Prologue to the Prophet Jonah.*

Chapter 6 Images

Jonah and the Whale by Pieter Lastman, 1621
Nineveh Adad gate (Fredarch/Wikimedia)
The Journeys of Jonah; satellite map courtesy of NASA
Jaffa (Seth Aronstam/Shutterstock)
Phoenician ship, National Museum of Beirut (NMB/Wikimedia)
Dice (Anamaria Todor/Shutterstock)
Sperm whale (Martin Prochazkacz/Shutterstock)
Nineveh archaeological site (Levi Clancy/Wikimedia)
Sennacherib, Mount Judi near Cizre, Turkey (Timo Roller/Wikimedia)
Jonah Preaching to the Ninevites by Gustave Doré, 1866
Goat and tent (Paul H. Wright)
Castor-oil plant (Natalia Nosova/Shutterstock)
Jonah fresco, Catacomb of Marcellinus and Peter, Rome, 4th century AD

Chapter 7

THE STORY OF ESTHER

Esther 1–10

THE BOOK OF Esther narrates the last of the great stories of the Old Testament. The action is set in the court of the Persian king Ahasuerus (a.k.a. Xerxes I), far from the land of Israel, a few decades after the Jews began to return to Jerusalem from exile in Babylon. The story exposes the challenges they faced learning to live away from their homeland, embedded in a foreign culture and under the political authority of someone else. Many Jews chose to not return to Jerusalem with Ezra and Nehemiah but remain as minorities in places that all too often were prone to treat them with suspicion and mistrust (the fate of minorities everywhere).

Esther's story is told with great flair, more so than many other Bible stories. In it, we find intrigue, irony, conviction, revenge, and even comedy. The Persian king, wrapped in the majesty of his throne, acts as a stooge (not to be sacrilegious to the text, but there probably isn't a better word to describe the events as they unfold). We see delicious turns of fortune, ones that the descendants of his Jewish subjects still enjoy as they retell the story today. The hero is Esther, a Jewish foreigner in a pagan land, whose beauty wins her a position in the royal court but whose resolve to die on behalf of her people not only saves the Jews from destruction but also has enshrined her memory as a noble heritage for all. Both how the story is told and what it reveals about us and God engage us to enter the story's dialogue and learn something quite personal in the process.

Scholars are keen to debate the extent to which the story of Esther is actual history. The narrative, many feel, is told in a way that is too good to be true. Esther has been categorized as a Persian court tale, a historical novel, a burlesque comedy(!), wisdom literature, satire embellished with comic art, an exercise in deadpan humor, a damsel-in-distress fairytale, a Midrash Haggadah (a fanciful Jewish tale with a timeless message), an extended parable, and an origin story for the festival of Purim—any or all of which are wrapped around a historical core. It is true that the events of the story of Esther are not mentioned in any other contemporary ancient text, but this is the case for most of the biblical record.

We can be sure, in any case, that the author of Esther intends his work to be read as history, and he includes all sorts of corroborating details to that end. Clearly the author knows much about the customs and architecture of the Persian royal court, its lavish decoration, and the equally lavish behavior of its residents—many of which are confirmed by archaeological discoveries, ancient Persian texts, and the writings of the Greek historian Herodotus who lived not long after the events of Esther took place.[1] (Herodotus was fascinated by the Persians, no doubt because they fought against Greece for world dominion during his lifetime.)

The Bible's description of Ahasuerus is consistent with what we know otherwise about the king: someone who was chauvinistic and headstrong (but weren't they all?), with a soft spot for lavish banquets, extravagant gifts, and generally the finer things of life. Throughout the story, the biblical writer makes sure to provide explanations for readers who may not be familiar with life in a Persian court, such as that the laws of the Medes and Persians cannot be repealed (Est. 1:19), a person can't enter the king's gate in sackcloth (Est. 4:2), and above all, no one (not even the queen) can approach the king's throne unless he holds out his golden scepter (Est. 4:11). Yet the author knows that readers who are unfamiliar with the ways of Persia will nevertheless resonate with the story, since Jews living outside their homeland (as well as a good many within) knew full well that threats to their very existence were never far from hand. Throughout, everything seems to be ratcheted up a notch or two, but this is the prerogative of an author who has something essential to say.

Scholars also debate the purpose of the book. In our English Bibles, Esther is the last in the sequence of books that provide a chronological account of the history of ancient Israel: the books of Joshua through Esther. This prompts us to read the story as a culmination of the mighty acts of God on behalf of his people, waiting only for his revelation in Jesus Christ. In the Hebrew Bible, however, Esther is placed in a group of books called the Writings, which includes Psalms, wisdom literature, and some late historical books (Ezra, Nehemiah, and Chronicles). In this collection, Esther is the last of a group of five books, or scrolls: Ruth, Song of Solomon, Ecclesiastes, Lamentations, and Esther. These five scrolls are each read annually on different important feast or fast days in the Jewish year; for Esther, it is the festival of Purim, which occurs in the last month of the Jewish calendar (Est. 9:20–32). This has prompted many scholars to conclude that the book of Esther was written to provide a historical explanation for Purim. The Old Testament provides an origin story for only one other feast: Passover, the springtime festival that opens the Jewish year commemorating the exodus from Egypt (Ex. 12). Together, Passover and Purim, bookending the Jewish year, remember historic events critical for the existence of the Jews: their birth out of the pangs of Egypt, and their survival, while in exile, from the threat of an empire-wide pogrom.

Megillah Esther (scroll of Esther), c. 19th century

Unlike the account of Israel's exodus from Egypt in which God's name and his miracles cannot be missed, the story of Esther nowhere mentions God. Neither do the land of Israel, Jerusalem, the temple, Torah, prayers, or God's covenant appear anywhere in the story. Nor are there visions or dreams (the stories of Joseph and Daniel, also set in foreign courts, at least include these). A quick read may suggest that Esther is just a nationalistic story, one of partisans struggling to survive by their own clever devices. This possibility was already felt by Jewish readers not long after the book was written. When the Old Testament was translated into Greek (the Septuagint) a short time later, the translators added over one hundred verses to the story elaborating Esther's religious devotion and that of Mordecai, her older cousin and advisor. In the first century AD, the Jewish historian Josephus added further material to make God even more visible in the story. All of this tells us that from the beginning, readers have been wrestling with the question, "Where is God in the crises of life or, for that matter, in day-to-day affairs?"

Other questions about the book have also troubled readers, especially its description of the Jews' triumph in killing their enemies (Est. 9:1–17). More to our liking is God's plan that Israel be a blessing to others, not kill them—a role of reconciliation celebrated in the last half of the books of Isaiah and Jonah where even Israel's enemies respond to God in peace. In the story of Joshua, the Israelites killed many Canaanites in the promised land, but at least the goal then was to provide a homeland free from influences of idolatry and immorality that would pull Israel away from God. The story of Esther, however, ends with Jews killing gentiles *outside* the land of Israel. We might posit that Esther was accepted as Scripture because Jews facing such great anti-Semitism outside of Israel knew that their very survival depended on a decisive response, an act of resistance. Jesus exhorts us to love our enemies in the face of threats to ourselves, our heritage, and our way of life by turning, he said, the other cheek (Matt. 5:38–48). The apostle Paul urges us to be transformed by Christ rather than "conformed to this world" (Rom. 12:2). Exactly *how* to resist threats and injustices to ourselves or to others, boots on the ground, in light

Queen Esther (Hugues Merle, 1875)

of each of these teachings remains a challenge many of us have trouble overcoming, much of the time.

The World of Esther and Xerxes I

Themes in the Story of Esther

God acts behind the scenes.

The book of Esther is unique in the Old Testament in that God's name is never mentioned anywhere, nor is it invoked in prayer by anyone in the story. Even so, no pious Christian or Jew would read the story thinking that its events are lucky happenstance or due to the cleverness of Mordecai and Esther alone. Rather, Esther's story is testimony that God's providential power is implicit in ordinary events, even when his presence is neither obvious nor seen.

God directs events offstage frequently in the Bible, even as his people struggle through situations that confront them. Many of these folks begin their stories fresh and green, such as the foreigner Ruth, the shepherd boy David, or the obedient girl Esther. And even as they gain skill and influence as their stories unfold, we see that each, personally, has no more real control over the outcome of events facing them than do the rest of us. We don't have to read very far into the grand narrative of the Bible to see that the lack of God's active presence in any biblical storyline is no indicator of the reality of his presence. And as the story of Esther culminates the narrative of the Old Testament, we are reminded that human cunning and desire, even at the highest levels, cannot overcome the providential will of God.

God is present with his people, even when they are in a strange place in life.

Much of the Old Testament emphasizes the importance of Israel living at home in a land centered on Jerusalem and the temple. But what happens when God's people live elsewhere (either by exile or by choice), when the temple no longer stands, when there is no king or army to protect their interests, and when they are overwhelmed by ways of life that are contrary to everything they hold dear, not to mention what is right in the eyes of God? This is the situation of the people of Israel after the Babylonians destroyed Jerusalem in 586 BC. The prophet Isaiah speaks of distant lands eventually hearing Torah instruction and the nations streaming to Zion in peace (Isa. 2:2–4; 48:12–16; 60:1–14). But what about the nitty-gritty times when the nations are hostile, and Israel isn't at home? How do we follow Jesus when it seems that everyone around us doesn't? Stories of Joseph, Daniel, and Esther—all of whom rise to prominence in a foreign court—show us that God's people remain under his covenantal care no matter where they might be.

Faithful living arouses suspicion and distrust.

Those of us who believe in the power of God to change lives are confronted by the reality that people often see a life lived in line with the claims of God as, well, weird. We are called to be different, not weird, but this doesn't change perceptions. In the story of Esther, trouble for the Jews starts when Mordecai, unlike the rest of the king's servants, refuses to prostrate himself before Haman (Est. 3:2). Mordecai is different; when he won't comply, Haman's arrogance feeds misrepresentations, which arouse suspicion, which then leads to an all-out extermination order from the powers that be. Here lies the story's brutality but also its insight into the innate, insidious nature of us all. Esther's story may be an extreme case (though perhaps not so extreme, given the propensity for pogrom and Holocaust ever since), but threat and hope for deliverance whenever we are persecuted for the sake of the gospel is not (Matt. 5:11).

We may be here "for such a time as this."

The story of Esther transforms our hero from a passive woman whose value to others is in her looks to a decisive force whose actions save an entire people. Her defining moment is not when she assumes royal power as queen but when, accepting the reality of self-sacrifice, she chooses to identify with her people. Esther is one of the Bible's greatest examples of resolve in spite of great temptations to remain silent (to be specific, in spite of very practical reasons for her to do so). She shows us that, in the midst of terrible conflict and tragedy, individual acts of greatness, through the grace and power of God, are most pronounced when we leave behind "what can I possibly do" to grasp "I am here for such a time as this" (cf. Est. 4:14).

Events in the Story of Esther

The King's Foolish Feast ESTHER 1:1–22

At a sumptuous banquet for ranking officials, King Ahasuerus summons Queen Vashti to parade before them. After Vashti refuses, the king banishes her from her position, then declares a kingdom-wide edict requiring all women give honor to their husbands.

Most scholars identify Ahasuerus with Xerxes I, son of Darius the Great, king of the Persian Empire from 485 to 465 BC. He reigned over the largest empire the world had yet known, "from India to Ethiopia" (Est. 1:1), the Indus River valley to upper (southern) Egypt. The events of the story of Esther begin in the third year of his reign, 483 BC, about sixty years after the edict of Cyrus the Great, founder of the Persian Empire, allowing the Jews to return to Jerusalem from their Babylonian exile (2 Chron. 36:22–23). In spite of Cyrus's edict, many Jews remained behind, either choosing to not return because they had started to feel at home in the cities of Babylon and Persia or didn't have the means to do so. The year 483 BC also corresponds to Xerxes's great war council prior to his invasion of Greece that ended with the battle of Thermopylae.[2] The book of Esther describes this council as an opulent 180-day gathering (Est. 1:3–4). The subsequent four-year beauty contest to prepare candidates to be the new queen must have taken place during Xerxes's absence from Persia for that war (Est. 2:1–12, 16). Though he was king of the largest empire the world had known, Ahasuerus is portrayed in the story of Esther as someone very much unaware of the happenings and trends in his kingdom, malleable by the intrigues of others, and a bit of a stooge.

Xerxes I holding his scepter and staff

The drama of Esther's story takes place in Susa, one of Persia's five capitals and a splendid city located on the eastern end of the Babylonian plain at the foot of the Zagros mountains. Inscriptions found in Susa speak of Xerxes living there early in his reign, embellishing the city's architecture and decorations (cf. Est. 1:5–7). Both Nehemiah and for a time Daniel also resided in Susa (Neh. 1:1; Dan. 8:2). Archaeological excavations have uncovered much of the expansive royal quarters of Susa but "the court of the garden of the king's palace" (Est. 1:5), the setting for much of the intrigue in Esther's story, has not been identified.

The king's order during his feast that Queen Vashti parade her physical attributes for the enjoyment of the guys can come only from a man with great power greatly impaired by drink (Est. 1:8, 10). And why can't the king ask his own queen to come to the party himself? Why does he need a full commission of seven private eunuchs—all with names that sound strange and rather pompous to Hebrew readers—to offer the invitation? Does this set the stage for the grand panoply of court (and the prerogative of kings), or is it because Ahasuerus knows Vashti will refuse his ridiculous (and equally shameful) order, and he wants to avoid looking chauvinistic all by himself? The story doesn't say why Vashti refuses, though the reason seems rather obvious to readers. In any case, to mention her reasoning would detract from the point that she never should have been asked in the first place.

After banishing Vashti, the king's follow-up edict that all women must give honor to their husbands simply exposes his rash action to the entire kingdom. Irrespective of the cultural norms of the day (patriarchy in all its forms was very much alive in the Persian court), is this really something that can be legislated? In the world of Ahasuerus, men must be men, even if it takes a royal edict to make them so.

Ruins of the once-magnificent royal palace of Darius and Xerxes I (foreground) at Susa, Iran

Cyrus the Great had founded the Persian Empire when he conquered Media in 550 BC. His empire is remembered for its beauty, efficiency, and royal pomp. It is also remembered for autocratic authority clothed in the guise of law. "The laws of the Persians and the Medes … may not be repealed" (Est. 1:19) has become an idiom for rigid bureaucracy to this day. Knowing this up front in the opening scene of Esther's story prompts us to wonder how, in the midst of the main crisis later on, can an even more rash edict—to annihilate the Jews—be overcome.

For Vashti, the king's law means immediate banishment, and here she disappears from the story, exit stage left. Once sober, the king will remember her (Est. 2:1), but his hands are tied (gasp!) by the laws of the Medes and Persians, as if he isn't the sole ruler in a monarchy without parliamentary override. But the edict has gone out, and the king's honor (whether he really has any or not) is shielded by law.

As readers, we perhaps would like to see Vashti somehow brought back on stage at the end before the cast takes its final bow, redeemed and restored to favor, but this is not to be. Rather, she remains but an unfortunate tool, though the means by which Esther can appear, center stage. Like so many in the Bible's narrative—Abel, Hagar, Orpah, and the daughter of Jephthah to name just a few—Vashti's story is over before it really begins.

The New Queen ESTHER 2:1–23

Ahasuerus fills his harem with young women from across his realm. One of these is Esther, a Jew. He is most pleased with Esther and makes her his queen. Meanwhile, her guardian, cousin Mordecai, informs Ahasuerus of a plot on the king's life and the conspirators are hanged.

The Greek historian Herodotus recounts that the Persians had a habit of deliberating serious matters at banquets while drunk, then confirming them after they had sobered up, which pretty much describes Ahasuerus's actions.[3] First he is swayed by his nobles to banish Vashti, and next he listens to his young attendants to search high and low for a new queen. Persian queens normally were chosen from royal rank or family, so an empire-wide search seems odd. Perhaps the king's attendants, young men all, had their own desires in mind by suggesting the search.

Enter cousins Mordecai and Esther. Their names reflect the cultural world in which the story takes place. Mordecai is the Hebrew form of a common Persian name, *Mardukka*, derived from Marduk, the chief Babylonian deity. The name Esther derives from Ishtar, the chief female deity in the ancient Near East who was worshiped as the goddess of love and war. Esther's name is often held to mean "star," and this is probably because Ishtar was also identified with Venus, the morning star. Herodotus mentions only one queen of Xerxes, Amestris, a name that scholars note resembles the name Esther, but these are unlikely the same person since Herodotus also says that Amestris accompanied Xerxes on his campaign to Greece.[4] Like most ancient monarchs, Ahasuerus probably had many wives in addition to his queen. Esther's Hebrew name is Hadassah, meaning "myrtle," an evergreen plant with upright branches bearing fragrant leaves. This is fitting, since Esther, like the myrtle, has become a symbol of immortality and hope in Jewish tradition (cf. Isa. 55:13).

Myrtle blossoms

Mordecai is described as someone "sitting at the king's gate" (Est. 2:19, 21; 5:13; cf. 5:9; 6:10). Because a gate is a place where business was conducted and court was held in the ancient world, Mordecai likely holds an official position at court. Scholars suggest that he may have been a magistrate or judge. A Babylonian text mentions a certain Mardukka who was a Persian official during the reign of Xerxes and some scholars are tempted to identify him with Mordecai, but this is no more than hopeful speculation. Josephus voices a different opinion: Mordecai was "one of the chief men among the Jews."[5] In either case, this would make the orphan Esther, Mordecai's cousin, not just a commoner but someone who already has some standing in society. If so, and assuming she hides her Jewish identity (which she does; Est. 2:10, 20), this increases her chances of being chosen for the king's harem and as a candidate to become queen.

Throughout the book, Mordecai and Esther are identified as Jews, not Israelites (Est. 2:5; 3:4; 5:13). The terms *Israelite* or *Judean* are proper for identifying the people of God's covenant prior to their exile to Babylon in 586 BC, while *Jew*, derived from *Judean*, becomes their nomenclature only after the exile.

The king gathers up a large harem of beautiful young virgins from across his vast kingdom, then has sexual relations with a different lady (probably girl) each night, most for a one-night stand, until he finds the one in whom he delights (Est. 2:8, 12–14). To be fair we probably should imagine that he made his way through the entire harem before choosing his queen; otherwise, how would he know that Esther found more favor with him than any of the others (Est. 2:17)? The reader needs to decide the details, as well as just what Mordecai might be thinking as he paces outside all the while (Est. 2:11).

As the story unfolds, we see Esther first as someone accommodating to the circumstances at hand. She "was taken into the king's palace" (Est. 2:8). We are given no indication as to how willing she was to go or if she could have refused. Once inside, Esther hides her Jewish identity, hangs out in a harem, eats and dresses like a gentile, and loses her virginity to a pagan king, all without uttering a word in the biblical text. By comparison, Daniel and his friends, Esther's contemporaries, refuse to do anything that compromises their singular devotion to the Lord when they are held captive in Babylon (Dan. 1:1–21; 3:1–30; 6:1–28). Perhaps this makes Esther more true-to-life in the end. We might dare to be a Daniel but know that most of the time we find it easier to be an Esther. The decisions of Esther reflect what many Jews in antiquity must have faced as they came into long-term contact with the world outside the land of Israel, where the issues of life were no longer as cleanly insular as they were back home.

The Edict ESTHER 3:1–4:17

Mordecai refuses to bow to Haman, the king's second-in-command. Enraged, Haman convinces the king to issue an edict that all the Jews in his realm be executed on a certain day eleven months hence. Mordecai implores Esther to intercede.

Haman, the vizier of Ahasuerus and "the enemy of the Jews," is an Agagite (Est. 3:1, 10; 8:1; 9:10). Following the suggestion of Josephus and early Jewish tradition, most interpreters consider Haman a descendant of Agag, king of the Amalekites, the archetype of enemies of Israel who was defeated by Israel's first king, Saul (1 Sam. 15:1–33; cf. Ex. 17:8–16; Deut. 25:17–18).[6] The story is silent on how a descendant of Agag ends up in Persia, but when it comes to behavior, it is clear that the apple fell close to its ancestral tree. Mordecai the Jew refuses to bow to Haman. No reason is given, and none need be other than that he is a Jew. Haman's response is typical of anti-Semitic reactions through the ages (Est. 3:6–11).

After telling us that Haman decides to kill all the Jews of the empire and before relating how Haman brings the matter to the king, the narrator inserts a short note on casting lots (Est. 3:7). In the ancient world, people cast lots, sometimes shaped like modern dice, for several reasons. One purpose was to determine or foresee the outcome of future events. Haman's advisors cast lots before him every day for an entire year. Whether this is his general practice or he keeps trying for the right dots to come up, we cannot know, though in the end Haman feels confident enough in the outcome to approach the king. This note reminds us of the sovereignty of God, something Haman knows nothing about. Proverbs 16:33 tells us that "the lot is cast into the lap, but its every decision is from the Lord." (The Hebrew word for lot is *pur*, from which the name Purim, the festival celebrating the Esther story, is derived.)

Haman's speech to Ahasuerus turns a personal grudge into a pogrom (Est. 3:8–15). It's standard stuff for a holocaust: there is an element of the population that not only opposes the king but keeps to their own customs and laws; surely they are disruptive to the state and must be destroyed. It's all spoken through a smile of guile. Ahasuerus asks no details. Who are these people? What is Haman's source of information? How long has this been going on? Have they infiltrated the palace? Who really is affected? *And why haven't I heard of it before?* All of this is quite strange, given what we otherwise know of Persian bureaucratic efficiency and tolerance. On the other hand, by now the king has been humiliated at the Battle of Thermopylae and the last thing he needs is a fifth column undermining his country at home. And so, Haman and the king sit down to drink while they issue the vilest of edicts: "to destroy, to kill, and to annihilate all Jews, young and old, women and children, in one day" (Est. 3:13, 15).

Up to this point in the story Esther has always been obedient to the counsel of her older cousin Mordecai. But now she balks at approaching the king; her excuse is that if she is not summoned, she will be executed: "All the king's servants and the people of the king's provinces know that if any man or woman goes to the king inside the inner court without being called, there is but one law—to be put to death, except the one to whom the king holds out the golden scepter so that he [or she!] may live" (Est. 4:11). The custom of holding out the golden scepter for admission to see the Persian king is not attested anywhere other than in the story of Esther. Why Ahasuerus would treat his own queen the same way he treats everyone else who has petitions is unknown. Couldn't she just speak to him, we might suppose, over lunch?

Mordecai replies by playing all his cards; if Esther doesn't intervene, she's doomed anyway: "For if you keep silent at this time, relief and deliverance will rise for the Jews from another place, but you and your father's house will perish. And who knows whether you have not come to the kingdom for such a time as this?" (Est. 4:14). Her response echoes both fatalism and resolve: "I will go to the king ... and if I perish, I perish" (Est. 4:16).

The Tables Turned ESTHER 5:1–7:10

Esther holds a banquet for Ahasuerus and Haman, then invites them to another the next day. That evening Haman erects a gallows on which to hang Mordecai. When Esther informs the king that it is her people whom Haman plans to annihilate, the king has Haman hung on his own gallows.

The action in the narrative at this point now moves very rapidly. Esther goes to the king and, far from perishing, she immediately finds favor in his sight. Herodotus gives specific examples of the generosity of Darius I and

Xerxes I (Ahasuerus), who bestowed favors on individuals who performed heroic deeds on behalf of the king. These gifts included the right to rule over cities or provinces in the empire.[7] Yet the offer by Ahasuerus to give Esther up to half his kingdom prior to her asking for anything must be taken as an idiom expressing pompous gratitude rather than as a literal offer. Esther has no designs to rule half the kingdom, only to ask for the king's attendance at a banquet. And not only his presence, but also that of his unsuspecting vizier, Haman.

Meanwhile, Haman is erecting a gallows for Esther's cousin Mordecai. Capital punishment in the Esther story is performed by hanging on the gallows (Est. 2:23; 5:14; 7:10). The Hebrew word translated as gallows (*'etz*) means simply "tree" and suggests that the implement of execution was a stake, for impaling, as depicted on ancient Assyrian reliefs. Haman's gallows is 50 cubits (75 ft; 23 m) high, clearly excessive for the job. Its height may be exaggerated to mirror Haman's self-image or to make sure that everyone witnesses the spectacle. Late Rabbinic tradition mentions that the tree was cedar, which can grow over 75 feet tall.[8] Updating the idea for his first-century audience, Josephus says that in the story of Esther, the people hung were crucified on a cross.[9]

Assyrian relief of the siege and defeat of Lachish, depicting Judeans impaled on stakes (701 BC)

While all this is going on, Ahasuerus happens to read (or by divine providence?) about how Mordecai once exposed a plot against the king's life—an anecdote we learn about earlier in the narrative (Est. 2:21–23). All ancient kingdoms that were literate kept written records of a wide variety of matters relevant to the proper functioning of the state. The chronicles, a book of memorable deeds which Ahasuerus consults on his sleepless nights, is reminiscent of similar written records kept by the royal courts of Israel and Judah and by prophets commenting on the affairs of the king (Est. 6:1; 10:2; cf. 2 Sam. 1:18; 1 Kings 11:41; 22:39, 45; 1 Chron. 29:29; 2 Chron. 12:15; 20:34).

The query of Ahasuerus to Haman, "What should be done to the man whom the king delights to honor?" is delphic, ambiguous as to the one to be honored (Est. 6:6). Haman's smug aside, voiced to himself and to any reader within earshot—"Whom would the king delight to honor more than me?" (Est. 6:6)—is one of the clearest and most comical instances in the Bible of the reader knowing better than the actor. Other examples are the aged Sarah upon being told she will bear a child (Gen. 18:12), Joseph's brothers facing him in the Egyptian court (Gen. 42–45), Joshua before the trickster Gibeonites (Josh. 9), Boaz asleep with Ruth at his feet (Ruth 3), and Mary ("How will this be, since I am a virgin?" Luke 1:34)—all characters caught in a moment of incredulity or simply unaware of the magnitude of the events confronting them.

In a moment of painful irony, Mordecai, wearing the king's honor, is paraded through the streets of Susa, all the while knowing that he and his people still hang under the death warrant of the king. It is delicious irony that Haman is stuck with leading the parade.

Esther's great courage and cunning actions quickly turn the tables on Haman. At her second banquet, she reports to Ahasuerus that his empire-

The Triumph of Mordecai (Jean François de Troy, c. 1736)

wide death warrant is directed at her people and that the instigator is his trusted vizier, Haman. Yet Esther still doesn't reveal her true identity nor, incredulously, does the king ask her who her people are. In the words of the essayist Maurice Samuel, writing for a modern Jewish audience with a clear aside to Christian listeners: "Not that Ahasuerus was a Jew-hater; he was merely the kind of person who votes a Haman into office and then says: 'Buchenwald? I never heard of the place.'"[10]

Ahasuerus is angry, but perhaps he has learned from personal experience what rash decisions can mean. The tipping point comes quickly as he walks in on Haman who, in "the place where they were drinking wine," is falling on Esther's couch, begging for mercy (Est. 7:8). The already livid (and probably bloodshot) eyes of Ahasuerus quickly interpret Haman's posture as indicating something else. Shakespeare could turn a plot no better. To use a modern phrase, it is instant karma when Haman is hung on his own gallows.

The Victory ESTHER 8:1–10:3

Realizing that he cannot overturn his prior edict, the king issues another that gives the Jews the right to defend themselves on the day designated for their destruction. After their victory, the Jews institute the feast of Purim commemorating their triumph.

It is only after Haman, the enemy of the Jews, is dead that Ahasuerus knows what the readers have known from the beginning: the honored Mordecai who saved the king's life is a cousin of his queen, Esther, and that Esther is a Jew. Haman's wife, Zeresh, had already suspected this was so and that the Jews would eventually prevail (Est. 6:13—perhaps the narrator includes this aside as a hint that men should do more listening to their wives and less insisting that they kowtow to Ahasuerus's first edict; cf. Est. 1:20–22). In any case, once Ahasuerus also knows, he is quick to take steps to ally himself with the Jews' cause.

The property of Haman, an executed criminal, falls to the crown. Both Ahasuerus and Esther—the queen is now finally acting on the king's behalf—award it and Haman's office, now empty, to Mordecai. How far we have come from the royal treatment of Vashti in the opening scene! Ahasuerus follows up by allowing Mordecai to write an edict "as you please with regard to the Jews, in the name of the king," sealed and irrevocable, that will give them permission to defend their lives and property against "any armed force of any people"—including, we must believe, the Persian army—seeking to destroy them (Est. 8:7–14). That this might lead to civil war within the empire is not an issue when the salvation of the Jews is at stake.

The Jews across the Persian Empire use the victory over Haman as a springboard to destroy their enemies, "those who sought their harm … those who hated them" (Est. 9:2–5). Altogether they kill 500 men in the citadel of Susa (these must have been royal troops), another 300 in the city, 10 sons of Haman, and 75,000 of their enemies across the provinces. Are we to think that all 75,810 of them shared the convictions of Haman? Perhaps they already harbored hatred of the Jews and Haman's edict simply gave them license to act on their prejudices. In any case, the purpose of the Jews' response is existential: to gain the right to live, not to become enriched in the process, for we read several times that they do not lay hand "on the plunder" (Est. 9:10, 15–16). Josephus embellishes his retelling of the story by noting that some of the gentiles who feared Mordecai's decree had themselves circumcised (to look like Jews) and thereby managed to avoid danger.[11] In a time and place in which many Jews were assimilating *out*, Josephus recognizes the value of assimilating *in*.

Esther 9:20–32 contains formal language institutionalizing the celebration of Purim "throughout every generation, in every clan, province, and city" (v. 28). The date of the annual celebration is fixed to the fourteenth day of the Hebrew month of Adar, the day after the fateful day when the Jews defeated their enemies (Est. 3:13; 8:11–12; 9:1, 17). The victory is celebrated one day later in the capital, the walled city of Susa, perhaps because one day was not enough to complete operations against those who opposed the Jews who were living there (Est. 9:18–19). Jewish tradition holds that Purim is celebrated on the fifteenth day of Adar in every city that was walled in the days of Joshua, including Jerusalem, and on the fourteenth day of Adar everywhere else.[12] The celebration includes feasting and gladness, as well as gift giving to family members and to the poor (Est. 9:19, 22).

The fourteenth day of Adar, the last month of the Jewish calendar, is one full moon prior to Passover, the fourteenth day of Nisan. These two festivals that begin and end the year remember existential moments in Jewish history when God redeemed his people from certain destruction.[13] Celebrating both helps the Jews start each year in the freedom of redemption (Passover) and end it thankful that they have passed safely through whatever dangers it might have held (Purim), realizing throughout that while God's presence may not always be visible, it is certain nonetheless.

Esther Denouncing Haman to King Ahasuerus (Ernest Normand, 1888)

ESTHER IN LATER WRITINGS

In the third century BC, the Septuagint added over one hundred verses to the story of Esther to demonstrate the piety of Esther and Mordecai and to front God's active hand in orchestrating its events. The Septuagint made the Bible accessible to Greek-speaking Jews living in the Diaspora, helping them learn how they also might survive in threatening environments.

Esther's story seems to have been less important for Jews living in the land of Israel prior to the destruction of the temple by Rome in AD 70, as it is the only book of the Old Testament not found in the Dead Sea Scrolls at Qumran. Neither is it quoted nor alluded to in the New Testament, perhaps because of its foreign setting or lack of explicit mention of God. Yet Esther's importance rose steadily after AD 70, as the Jews once again were forced into direct contact with the gentile world. By the third century, an entire tractate (chapter) in the Mishnah was dedicated to the book and how to observe Purim.

The earliest reference to Purim outside of the book of Esther is in the book of 2 Maccabees.[14] There it is called Mordecai's Day and linked to the Jews' victory over the Seleucid-Greek general Nicanor, a key moment in the Maccabean war of independence in the second century BC. This bolstered the book's nationalistic themes in early Judaism. Ultimately two strands prominent in the story—piety and nationalism—combined in the minds of Jewish readers of Esther, holding her as an example of heroic self-preservation in the face of anti-Semitism. To quote Robert Gordis, "It is fundamental to the Jewish world-outlook that the preservation of the Jewish people is itself a religious obligation of the first magnitude."[15]

The book of Esther was not fully accepted as Scripture by Christians until the late fourth century AD, likely because it does not specifically mention God and because of its nationalistic fervor. The Protestant Reformers were equally troubled. Both John Calvin and Martin Luther denounced the book, and although both were prolific writers on Scripture, neither chose to write a commentary on Esther. Yet from the earliest days of Christianity, the story of Esther has been fertile ground for theologians seeking examples of moral fortitude for believers in Christ:

- Jerome and the church fathers generally saw Esther as an example of the church defending itself from "Hamans": persecution, iniquity, and Satan's desire that everyone—including all the "Mordecais" of the world—worship him.[16]

- St. Aphrahat the Persian (third century AD) encouraged believers who were under duress to persevere like Esther, then compared the persecution and glorification of Jesus to that of Mordecai.[17]

- *The Apostolic Constitutions*, an eight-volume text of Christian liturgy and church organization dating to the fourth century AD, includes several prayers of thanksgiving that seem to have originated as synagogue prayers prior to the time of the New Testament. The church fathers adopted these Jewish prayers but added lines about Christ to them (we enjoy a shared heritage). These prayers—some of which mention Esther and Mordecai—show that through the daily liturgy of the early church, Christians have been reminded of the mighty acts of God throughout history, and that all of his work is fulfilled in Jesus.[18]

We give thanks to you for all things, O Master Almighty,
because you have not forsaken us with your mercies and your compassions;
but generation after generation you save, rescue, lay hold of, (and) shelter.
For you laid hold of (people) *in the days of Enos and Enoch,*
in the days of Moses and Joshua,
in the days of the Judges,
in the days of Samuel and Elijah and of the prophets,
in the days of David and of the Kings,
in the days of Esther and Mordecai,
in the days of Judith,
in the days of Judah Maccabeus, and of his brothers,
And in our days you laid hold of us through your great High Priest, Jesus Christ your Child.
For even from the sword he rescued,
and from famine he delivered, having maintained (us);
from disease he healed,
and from an evil tongue he sheltered (us).

Study Questions

1. How does the book of Esther address the question "Where is God in the crises of life or, for that matter, in day-to-day affairs?"

2. How are the four main characters portrayed in the story: Ahasuerus, Mordecai, Esther, and Haman? Do you think these are fair characterizations? Why or why not?

3. Do you think that there were times when Esther had to compromise her values in order to gain and keep her position? What would you do if you were in her situation?

4. In what ways are the actions and attitudes of Haman typical of those who oppose God's people, be they Jews or believers in Jesus?

5. Considering God's plan that Israel should be a light to the nations, what are we to make of the Jews' triumph in killing their enemies that is recounted at the end of the story of Esther?

6. Have you had an experience where you feel that God prepared you specifically "for such a time as this"?

Chapter 7 Notes

1 For details, see Karen H. Jobes, "Esther 2: Extrabiblical Background," 170–175, in *Dictionary of the Old Testament: Wisdom, Poetry and Writings*, eds. Tremper Longmann III and Peter Enns (IVP Academic, 2008).
2 Herodotus, *Historiae*, 7.8.
3 Herodotus, *Historiae*, 1.133.
4 Herodotus, *Historiae*, 7.61, 114.
5 Josephus, *Antiquities of the Jews*, xi.198.
6 Josephus, *Antiquities of the Jews*, xi.209; Esther Rabbah 7.13; 9, 4; Targum Sheni on Esther 9.7.
7 Herodotus, *Historiae*, 3.138, 140; 8:85; 9:107.
8 Targum Sheni on Esther 9:7.
9 Josephus, *Antiquities of the Jews*, xi.208.
10 Maurice Samuel, *Certain People of the Book* (Union of American Hebrew Congregations, 1955), 18.
11 Josephus, *Antiquity of the Jews*, xi.285.
12 Mishnah, Megillah 1.1.
13 Paul H. Wright, ed., *Rose Guide to the Feasts, Festivals and Fasts of the Bible* (Rose Publishing, 2022), 67.
14 2 Maccabees 15:36.
15 Robert Gordis, *Megillat Esther* (The Rabbinical Assembly, 1974), 13.
16 Jerome, *Epistle*, 53.8; Glossa Ordinaria, Patrologia Latina 114.743.
17 Aphrahat, *Demonstrations*, 20.
18 Apostolic Constitutions 7.38.1–9; James Charlesworth, ed. *The Old Testament Pseudepigrapha* (Hendrickson, 1983), 685. Emphasis added by author.

Chapter 7 Notes

Esther before Ahasuerus by Giuseppe Bonati, c. 1650
Megillah Esther, 19th century, Iraq, The Jewish Museum
Esther before Ahasuerus by Hugues Merle, 1875
The World of Esther and Xerxes I; satellite map courtesy of NASA
Relief of Xerxes I, National Museum of Iran (Darafsh/Wikimedia)
Susa ruins (Poliorketes/Shutterstock)
Myrtle (LifeCollectionPhotography/Shutterstock)
Lachish relief from the wall of Sennacherib's palace in Nineveh, The British Museum (Mike Peel/Wikimedia)
The Triumph of Mordecai by Jean Francois de Troy, c. 1736
Esther Denouncing Haman to King Ahasuerus by Ernest Normand, 1888

Afterword

THE STORIES OF the Bible beckon us. Opening the cover of the Bible, we don a colorful dream coat, flush with a chance of success. Turning a page, we lay crushed with the weight of sackcloth, hearing news that is not of our doing. We hold up wide the hem of our robe, eager for more than mere gleanings. And we put on the full armor of Goliath, sure of our means of protection. Absorbed in the safety of accounts long ago, we forget that we are gazing into a mirror, and it's not a glass darkly. Or we turn away, preferring instead to be entertained, then close the cover for other things. "There is nothing new," says the Preacher, "under the sun" (Eccl. 1:9). The questions we ask of the people whom we meet on the pages of Scripture are in fact the questions we ask of ourselves. And like Mary, we carry them to the foot of the cross.

John ends his gospel by reminding us that there are many more stories about Jesus, and if they were all written down, "the world itself could not contain the books that would be written" (John 21:25). Imagine how many worlds it would take to contain books recording all the stories that could be told beginning with the garden of Eden. We are caught between wanting to know more and knowing that what we have is sufficient to know who Jesus is (John 20:30–31). Yet every time we read an unfamiliar portion of the Bible or reread a story that we already know, the Spirit of God seeks to impress something on us that will allow us to live with a greater understanding of God's significance for our lives. "I've read this once already" is not a claim that satisfies. Reread these stories again, and then launch yourself into others that grace the pages of the Bible. Keep a pencil and notebook handy, with a heart open to the Spirit of God to chart your way.

The journey has already begun.

Books by Paul H. Wright

Rose Guide to the Feasts, Festivals, and Fasts of the Bible

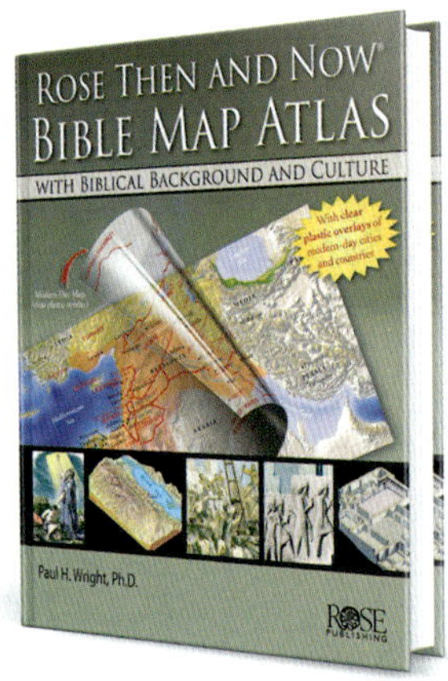

Rose Then and Now® Bible Map Atlas with Biblical Background and Culture

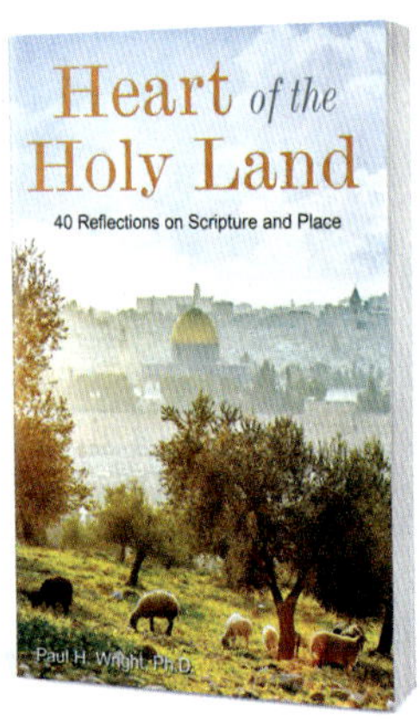

Heart of the Holy Land: 40 Reflections on Scripture and Place

Behind the Bible's Greatest Stories: Exploring the Culture, Context, and History of Famous Stories